ADVANCE PRAISE FOR
MOTHERS LOSING MOTHERS

"This book is like a hug from your mother. When my mother passed away I searched for something to read to comfort me and ease my pain. Now I have a warm blanket of understanding for myself and others. Randy put into words what is in our hearts and opened a door of healing for women. I was up the other night reading the book until about one or two in the morning because I was just so sad and it was just like having your best friend sitting right next to you – the comfort that I got from it, just knowing that I wasn't crazy, that my feelings were okay. It really is such a necessary book. I love it! Thank you Randy for sharing your experience and allowing others to feel they have someone to share the journey with."
                    Lorraine Kinslow, mother and daughter

"Congratulations, kudos, hats off! To do such a fine job on a topic so universal, but delicate and sensitive. You have opened the door to a necessary topic – the time of which has come! Thank you!"
                    Elena S. Whiteside, grandma!

 "Randy's book is a treatise about one the most cherished relationships of all – between mothers and daughters. All the stories read as an insight into the journey of that woman and her family, yet with a universal appeal. Randy's chapters are filled with wisdom and love that highlight the experience of knowing and loving one's mother. Having lost my own mother at a young age, I readily relate to the grief and growth this experience brought me, and still does dozens of years later. The stories told here will be jewels for all women to enjoy. *Mothers Losing Mothers* is a must read for any woman. Congratulations on creating a timeless book!"
                    Alice Baland, psychotherapist, speaker, daughter, and author of *Eat Up The Good Life*

"Your book put me in a reflective mood remembering great times with my mother and her mother during WWII (My father was in the Army.) My mother has been gone for almost 20 years now but the feelings are there and reflection is a soothing tool. I feel she is still touching my life and guiding me as my Guardian Angel. Your book sent me a 'healing touch' of memories. These memories I have used as I raised my two daughters and now have been blessed with two granddaughters. My mother is proud of all of us, I'm sure. Your hope for all of us mothers to 'appreciate the natural process of mourning and recovery that follows the death of your mother' is wonderfully expressed in your book. All the many unique experiences included in your book are a shared platform and provide some better tools to not 'hide from the task of letting go.'"

Penelope Mont, author of *What's Going to Happen to Me When I Die?* and other books on end of life issues

"Randy's book is an intimate insight into the profound love and bond that exist between mothers and daughters at all ages and into the transformative process that occurs at and after a mother's passing. It is somewhat surprising how similar and yet different the stories by women quoted in her book are – they offer a rare opportunity to share the joys, grief, and thoughts of those going through the process of coming to terms with a mother's death. The author is not only a daughter who has experienced her mother's death but an experienced counselor who has had the benefits of working with many mothers and daughters over the period of 25 years. She generously shares her insights and knowledge with her readers. This book can offer solace and advice to any woman or man going through a similar experience."

Joanna Infeld, writer, editor, and publisher, *Kora Press*

"I found *Mothers Losing Mothers* to be very interesting, insightful, and a worthwhile contribution to the literature on human interaction."

Robert E. Kay, M.D., psychiatrist (retired)

"Randy has done it again! She offers a collection of personal accounts of loss that we as mothers/daughters can relate to on many levels. These personal stories impart to us – the mothers/daughters – the strength and courage to persevere through our own course of grieving and ultimately embrace the loss of a beloved mother. We clearly see how this process can continually transform us into a new and inspired identity, one equipped with some wonderful qualities we recognize as our mother's spirit living on in us. Thank you so much Randy, for this valuable resource!"

Andrea Broido, daughter, mother, and opera singer

MOTHERS LOSING MOTHERS

COMFORT AND REASSURANCE IN YOUR TIME OF LOSS

Randy Colton Rolfe

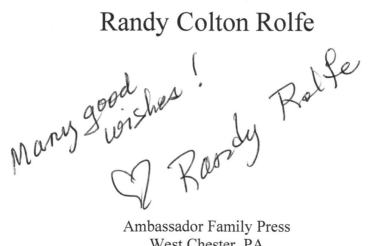

Many good wishes!

♡ Randy Rolfe

Ambassador Family Press
West Chester, PA

Mothers Losing Mothers:
Comfort and Reassurance in Your Time of Loss

ISBN-13: 978-1478106548
ISBN-10: 1478106549

Ambassador Family Press
West Chester, PA

I dedicate this book
To my mother and my grandmothers, now departed,
To my sister, to my husband and my children
Who gave me the gift of becoming a mother, and
To all mothers, who together pass on the gift of life.

Regardless of your relationship with your parents, you'll miss them when they're gone from your life.
MAYA ANGELOU

CONTENTS

Most mothers are instinctive philosophers.
HARRIET BEECHER STOWE

There would have to be something wrong with someone who could throw out a child's first Valentine card saying, "I love you, Mommy."
GINGER HUTTON

CHAPTER 1

MOTHERS LOSING MOTHERS: A SILENT PAIN

When I was twelve, my family and I were visiting a distant cousin, Cousin Odette, in the French countryside north of Paris. Cousin Odette was the perfect French lady to me, beautiful, elegant, energetic, and living in what seemed to me a small castle, what the French call a chateau. It was built of stucco and wood, with courtyard and walled garden, and doves cooing in the belfry. Her castle was named Banthelu, after the nearby village. Odette was mayor, and everyone knew her. She loved presiding over the frequent village festivals.

That evening she took us on a tour of her home, grand dining room girded with antiques, narrow turrets, great winding staircase, secret passageways, and a hall of mirrors, where she swore she had a ghost, a handsome knight, who made himself visible from time to time. She said his name was Guillaume.

As dark night fell over the quiet little castle, we enjoyed a sumptuous homemade French dinner and we children were sent off to bed. While I lay snugly in bed under a luxurious down comforter, surrounded by thick grey walls with dark tapestries hanging on them and a high ceiling above me, I listened to my parents' animated chat with Odette as it echoed up the stairway. I couldn't make out the words but the sounds felt wonderfully comforting and reassuring.

Then suddenly, for the first time in my life, it occurred to me that they would not always be there. It would not always be like this. The talk of ghosts must have affected my mind. I realized my mother and father would one day not be with me to comfort and reassure me. Someday I would be without them. I was terrified.

We would not always be the same: Me the daughter, they the parents, laughing, talking, traveling, living, always having each other. Here we were in a castle which was centuries older than any of us would ever be. One day their voices would not echo through the castle. I was able to go to sleep only by reassuring myself that such a time was far, far in the future and I would be an adult, able to cope with it.

Now, indeed, it has happened. The future has arrived and they are all gone. The castle is empty. In my struggle to identify the torrent of feelings in the aftermath of my mother's recent passing, the image of a suddenly empty castle seized my mind's eye. A flood of tears overcame me, having finally found a visual image for my feelings. Having grown up watching Disney princesses like Sleeping Beauty and Cinderella and singing *Snow White* songs by the wishing well my father had build for me of stone, the image hit home. The castle of my youth was now empty and I had to come to terms with it as best I could.

An empty castle

Just as we have come to call it our "empty nest" when we must adjust to our children leaving their childhood home and us behind, so I think of the "empty castle" when we must adjust once again to our mothers leaving their earthly life and us behind. Just like the empty nest seems so quiet and still compared to the days of parenting, so the empty castle seems somber and strange compared to the days of having a mother always at the other end of the phone.

It seems more and more that my memories of my mother are associated with the physical items with which she surrounded herself, the things she touched and treasured, and the things with which she liked to occupy herself. The castles our mothers built around us as their young princesses were a treasury of tastes, smells, sounds, visions, and physical manifestations of who she was. But in her last days, when she was in the hospital room, she had none of those things around her except for her comb and her purse. Her loved ones, me and my sister Kim and her life partner, second love of her life, were all she had then to comfort her.

Each night my sister and I would leave the hospital room hoping things could get better. More tests, more prayers, more questions from our mother, more mixed messages from doctors. Finally they knew there was no more they could do. The hospice specialists walked us through the last days to come and explained that it was good for our mother to hear it all. She was at last on painkillers to ease her transition. But no one knew when it would come, except perhaps our mother.

I believe no one can be fully prepared for their mother's death. No matter how long it has been approaching, no matter how many books you have read about it, experts on hospice or gerontology you may have consulted, talks on palliative care you may have attended, prayers you have said, friends you have known who have experienced the loss, or conversations you have shared with your mother, it is still a reality that can only be grasped when it has actually happened.

We don't really know how we will react

Will we cry, not cry, scream, go dead silent, lose our appetite, forget to sleep, go numb, hide our pain, wish the doctors had done a better job, call our children, call our friends, not call our friends, worry about funeral arrangements, pray someone else will do all that, feel relief that the final ordeal is over, feel regret we did not say more, or maybe less, replay the last days over and over in our minds without knowing why?

What does our new life look like? Can we imagine it without her? Should we try to imagine it without her?

Was it the way she wanted? Would she have preferred it be quicker or slower? Would she have preferred to make her passage with more people around or fewer or with different people or none?

And how will we remember her over the years? How will her grandchildren remember her over their years? Should we have brought them in to see her or not?

All of these questions want answers. But we can't call our mother to chat about our mind-meanderings anymore. We must wander the castle alone. For the first time.

How did our mother handle her own mother's death over time? Will I be the same or different? Can I get any clues there?

No one seems to understand

No matter how sympathetic our loved ones are or how close the society at large views the mother-daughter relationship, it still seems that no one really can understand the depth of the sadness. They don't understand how habits can change overnight, how small events can trigger emotional responses where there were none before, and how, most unusual of all, we have a persistent sense of absence, of something profoundly important missing from the context of our lives. It seems as if it is in the natural order of things to lose our mothers after we have become mothers ourselves, and even grandmothers ourselves.

It seems impossible for others to grasp that in many ways this makes it harder rather than easier to accept and to process all the emotions, memories, and shifts in perception which come to us on the death of our mothers, indeed exactly because of our maturity and our personal experience of being an adult woman and mother.

Others rarely understand or appreciate the complexity of what we are going through. Our husbands or partners do their best to comfort us, give us space, and offer their sympathy and help with daily chores and functions. Yet the popular expectation is that it is the normal course of things to lose your mother once you are a mother yourself and the generations continue. Why is it so hard? Once the shock is over and the funeral is past and the condolences are accepted and the mother's affairs are set in order, life goes on, right?

Why can you still get sudden wet eyes at a scene which reminds you of your childhood when you haven't thought about that time of your childhood in over 30 years? Why are you less patient? Why do things you cared about seem less important? Why are other silly little things taking on more importance?

Those around you have a hard time understanding. So many people are losing their parents these days, as the baby boomers reach age 50, that the media has finally started to talk about losing your parents and what is normal for grieving. Are we supposed to "return to normal" in 6 months or 12? Is our "healing" and "new insight" supposed to set everything straight on a new path of maturity?

Or are we allowed to dwell in our grief as long as it takes to "feel" like focusing again on our daily lives, and how do we carry on in the meantime until that happens?

Mothers Losing Mothers is a way for me to add some value to the world of human experience by documenting our feelings and thoughts at this unique time in our lives. My mother was all about improving the lives of the world's peoples through education and understanding. This is in a sense one way of continuing her work.

A pain we have never felt before

The essential problem which we face as a mother who has lost the mother she loves is to deal with a pain we have never felt before and then to get on with life in a life-affirming way in the midst of the full realization, either new or remembered, that we are here just for a short time, that every day matters, and that our legacy is only what our progeny – that is, our mother's grandchildren – will make of it.

This event forces us to wrestle with many questions, even the ultimate question, what is it all for?

Depending on your religious, spiritual, or philosophical perspective, most likely derived from or in reaction to your mother's perspective, we each must find our own answers.

Combined with the overwhelming responsibilities which fall to a daughter-mother who has just lost her beloved mother, these questions can really change your approach to many aspects of your life, from marriage, exercise, self-image, friendships, and aging, to parenting, priorities, and existence itself. The intent of this book is to help you take the time to explore all these life aspects with a wonderful group of compassionate women who have gone through the experience themselves.

When I originally conceived of this book, which idea came as a total surprise to me, I thought I would lay out a process which a reader could follow to help her deal with all the tasks, responsibilities, feelings of confusion, overwhelm, abandonment, and questions which come and go at this time. But I soon discovered that each person's process is unique to her and each person's story is different.

The root of healing is in the story itself

As I began to interview other women who were going through the first year since the death of their mother, I slowly came to realize that the root of the healing process was in the story itself. So my intent today is to offer you the priceless resource of sharing with other women who know where you are and what you are going through.

For me, as it turned out, the solution was talking with people who could understand what I was feeling. I hope you will discover by reading the stories in *Mothers Losing Mothers* that you can think of the women whose stories you are hearing as sisters, the way my sister was to me. I would have had a much harder time without her. I don't want to imagine what it would have been like if she had not been sharing this experience with me. But I know women in that situation, who are going it alone, and I don't want them to have to do that.

Women all around are sharing the same loss

After my mother's death, as I was trying to continue on with life as usual, I soon discovered that several friends at the local business networking meetings I attended were experiencing the loss of their mothers at the same time I was. Then I heard from several of my high school classmates with whom I had stayed in touch. They had also just lost their mothers. And then several business associates from other parts of the country, whom I knew through my independent consultant business with Nikken, Inc., a global wellness technologies company, shared with me that they too were going through this difficult time. I discovered that women all around me of a certain age were experiencing the same loss.

I found that in talking even just casually at first with these women, there was a knowing we shared that no one else could comprehend. Often we talked about how little understanding there was in the culture at large. Often we talked about the last days and all the Monday morning quarterbacking we were doing or trying not to do. Or we would talk about how everything else was on hold while we wrestled with matters of our mother's estate or how to deal with new or changed priorities. Or we talked about relatives who didn't seem to care as much as we did or who felt helpless not knowing how to help. Our chats ran the gamut.

Sometimes we would commiserate about the awkward questions or comments of others: "How old was she? Oh, I guess then she had a good life, and you were certainly a great daughter to her."

I knew I had said such things myself to others who were mourning a loved one.

Now I knew this was not very helpful. "Tell me about it," would have been much more helpful and became my new response. I certainly wasn't looking for counseling clients; it was just that now I knew better how to give some friendly comfort.

When I realized this need for mothers to share with other mothers when they lose their mothers, I decided to interview a few of these wonderful women at some length and draw some conclusions from their stories and thoughts. But once I had assembled their interviews, I realized that their stories were much more valuable to other mothers if kept in their own individual voices, with each unique story told as a whole. My analysis became superfluous. Instead I just wanted to share the stories, while emphasizing along the way a few key points: that this time is difficult by nature, that we are not alone, that it's an emotional process, that we can be misled at this vulnerable time, and that it does get better, even great, if we trust the natural process.

I made no attempt to achieve a scientific sampling of mothers bereft of their mothers. Rather I chose to keep it more personal and subjective, like the process of mourning itself. I interviewed Carol, the wife of a friend from my childhood. I interviewed two independent colleagues in the Nikken, Inc., business, Elaine from Western Pennsylvania and Mary Ann from Vermont. I interviewed two of my friends, Susan and Pam, who were my classmates for many years at Shipley, the private girls' school we attended together in Bryn Mawr, Pennsylvania. And I interviewed my sister Kim, asking her the same questions I had explored with each of the other women, even though we had talked many times already of course about most of these topics. Then I asked myself the same questions I had asked my guest sharers and told my own story.

Diverse stories but with the same heart

Even within this small group with whom I already had personal connections, there was a great diversity among their stories. Each has a different story. Some were there at the time of death, others were not. Some faced more responsibilities after the death than others. Some faced a sudden death while others did not.

Meanwhile each person shares her story of love and loss with a great sensitivity, which does more to show what we all have in common as we go through this experience than any analysis I could make. All share the pain, sadness, emotion, and cascade of feelings which each of us experiences. And their different voices touch different strings in your heart, so that you can find the solace and comfort that you uniquely want and need.

I was also pleased to discover how much gratitude these women expressed, simply for having the opportunity to tell their story and to hear bits of mine. This response confirmed the great value of sharing our stories and hearing the stories of others. It demonstrated the need for this book and the benefits it can offer to you. I hope also that *Mothers Losing Mothers* will be a favorite gift for caring friends to give to a mother who has lost her mother.

By engaging with these women and their movement from tragedy to transformation and triumph, I believe you will find the courage and support to open up generously to your own story and reach new ground you might have only dreamed of before.

A time of tragedy, peril, and transformation

What I would emphasize to you here is the sometimes unrecognized magnitude of this event in your life, and also the fact that you are not alone in feeling how impactful this event is, no matter what messages you may be getting from society, friends, family, or advisers. It is a perilous time, but also indeed, a time of transformation. You must give it the time and attention it deserves. Not only can things fall apart around you physically, but the emotional results can literally be life threatening if you try to ignore the impact of your mother's passing.

Instead, honoring your deep and complex relationship with your mother and your profound appreciation for all she represented to you now that you are a mother and maybe also a grandmother like she became, puts you squarely on the path to a new serenity, sense of gratitude, and appreciation for life itself.

In *Mothers Losing Mothers*, I have multiple purposes. First, I seek to comfort you with the shared stories of women who have just gone through the same sad events that you and I have. Second, I hope to honor our mothers for all they have meant to us. Third, I wish to alert our communities to the supreme importance of mothers for the future of humanity. Fourth, I intend to show others who know and care about women going through this passage how they can best help. And fifth, I desire to continue the efforts of our mothers to create a better world through understanding and compassion.

I hope ultimately you will want to share with others these important points about mourning the loss of our mothers:

- The loss of our mothers is meant to hurt, by divine and natural imperative.

- You are not alone in experiencing this event and feeling its great impact.
- Mourning is a feeling process which you must honor and allow to proceed.
- There are pitfalls of distraction, self-medication, and misdiagnosis.
- There is light at the end of the tunnel, a renewing and spiritual light.

My hope is that in these pages:

- You will discover that you need not feel alone, because so many are going through the same experience, in fact more than ever before in history, sharing in many ways a unique experience.
- You will come to understand how your suffering may feel augmented by the failure of society to appreciate the importance of mothers, their lives, and their deaths, so that society doesn't hear your pain.
- You will see revealed the power of stories to show you new ways to feel your feelings and to show you that your feelings are important, normal, and natural and need acknowledgment and tender loving care.
- You will find hope, comfort, and reassurance, knowing that though it is real and profound, your sadness will evolve and your life can be transformed in a good way, from tragedy to triumph, through seven powerful stages.
- You will come to appreciate that many of today's woes are caused by a misunderstanding of our feelings and life passages and you will be able to avoid trying to fix what doesn't need fixing.
- You will receive a myriad of tools from the stories you hear to bring you to a new state of gladness and gratitude, transformation and triumph, trusting in

your own natural timing to benefit from the gift and legacy of your mother and motherhood.
- You will come to appreciate that your unique story is part of your contribution to the creative process of the human family and it can be of great value not only to your healing but also to your loved ones, to the people you care about, and to others you may not even know.

Each of these ideas will be expanded in later chapters which are interspersed between the stories of women like you who are mothers losing mothers.

Who can benefit

If you are a mother who has recently lost her mother, I hope that you will find a kind of sisterly support in the stories you will be hearing here. These stories can make all the difference as you go through the process of reinventing your physical and emotional life without your mother here.

Many millions of women who have children themselves are facing the prospect of losing their mothers in the next ten years. If you are a mother who has lost her mother, you will appreciate that you are not alone and you will gain consolation, knowledge, and understanding from other women who have shared the same loss and survived it, and who can give you hope of future comfort and peace.

If you are one of the many millions who are facing the passing of your mother in the next few years and are perhaps in the process of helping her to enjoy her life and her health as long as she can, you will gain wisdom and support from women who have been through the experience, and who can show you that if they did it you can too.

If you have a relative, friend, or someone you care about who has lost their mother or is facing the prospect of loss, you will better understand how to be there for them and support them on all levels.

You may be the child of a mother losing a mother. If your mother is acting differently or is hiding her feelings or is being strong for your sake, you will gain a deeper appreciation of what all this means to your mother and how you can help her and take care of yourself as well.

If you are a caregiver for an elderly woman who has children and grandchildren, you will acquire the tools you need to be sensitive and helpful to her family as well as to your ward as she departs.

You may be a doctor, nurse, or other health care provider who treats elderly patients. From the stories in this book you will get a vital snapshot of the multiple reactions families can have to the loss of a mother and grandmother, even if she is elderly and departing at her normal life expectancy.

If you are a health care provider who tends to the physical, mental, or emotional needs of women in their 40s, 50s, or 60s, you may find this book helpful in appreciating one of the generally unrecognized stresses many of these women are experiencing, caring for and saying goodbye to a beloved mother.

If you are the husband of a mother losing a mother, you will have the insights you need, which cannot really be obtained any other way than by hearing others' stories, to be the support and companion your loved one wishes you to be.

For all who are concerned with the proper treatment of our elderly as they go through the final phase of their lives, there is no greater benefit than to hear from their daughter-mothers what this event means to them, what are their hopes for their mother's final days, how it will impact their lives, and how they can find their way through it, make sense of it, and ultimately benefit with new wisdom and understanding, for their own lives and for the lives of their children, grandchildren, communities, and the world.

To get the most benefit from *Mothers Losing Mothers*, open your heart to the caring words you will read here. This book is for those who loved their mothers, not for those who had poor or non-existent relationships.

Who may not receive any benefit

If you believe the death of your mother can't or shouldn't have much impact once you are already out of the house and a mother yourself, you will miss the deep comfort and opportunity for growth that the stories in this book afford you.

Likewise, someone who wants to rely on pills to cover the sadness, mourning, depression, doubts, loneliness, stress, or anxiety that can follow a loved one's death will not receive much benefit.

If you feel you can handle your pain all by yourself without sharing your feelings and thoughts and without listening and benefiting from the experiences of others, then I urge you to reconsider, or please pass this book on to someone who wants social support.

If you choose to deny the impact of your mother in your life and the likely impact of her death on your life as a woman, wife, mother, or grandmother, the benefits of this project may escape you.

If you have bought into the grin-and-bear-it philosophy that we should all feel happy all the time and take life and death in stride, then I might mention that suppressing sad feelings eventually leads to suppression of happy ones too. The stories you hear here may give you a broader range of appreciation for the beauty, wonder, and profound lessons of life.

Perhaps you have already explored one or more of these approaches and found them wanting. If so, keep open to another way, and you will reap unforeseen benefits from the stories in *Mothers Losing Mothers*.

The passing of generations

While driving in my car just this morning, I heard an interview with a woman who was celebrating her 103rd birthday. She said that she attributed her longevity to always being the best she could be, loving people deeply, and finding the good side of life. But she also said that until her husband died when she was 62, she had always defined herself as his wife and as mother of their children, and that she never dreamed of being as free as she feels now at 103.

I thought how different our generation is from hers, and how the next generation is more different still. I've never defined myself as a wife or mother. It's a privilege to be a wife and a mother and I adore it and I wouldn't exchange it for anything in the world, but it's not who I am. I knew these roles would be at the core of how I live my life but they don't define me.

The next generation seems to specifically want to define themselves before they even commit to being a wife or mother, which I think is a step even further away from our mothers and grandmothers. As you will hear later in this book, our generation has a unique relationship with our mothers and unique responses as they leave us.

From over 25 years of experience as a speaker, author, and counselor on family issues, I knew even before my mother died that the death of a mother is life-changing, if not life-shattering. I found that among my clientele, there were often mature, highly functioning, loving mothers who still carried pain from unhealed wounds from the experience of their mother's death, even when their mothers had lived out their full life expectancy and beyond. I helped many women deal with the emotional, physical, and spiritual consequences of their relationships with their mothers, often even long after their mother had died. I saw the range of feelings they had, and I was pleased to be able to help them work through their feelings in a way that left them stronger and happier.

What I found most often was that they had not realized how profoundly their mothers had affected their sense of themselves, as wife, mother, or woman. With their mothers gone, their sense of self was often shaken and needed to be re-evaluated or even re-created. It became clear to me that a mother is not only critical in the early years of life, but she remains a force in our lives long after we are adults and mothers ourselves, and when she is gone the gap must be addressed and bridged for us to feel good about who she was and who we are in this world.

The greatest help

In helping these clients, my approach was to help them rethink their relationship with their mother, to listen to their story, and to help them now look at it from the perspective of their own experience as a mother. As they told their stories to me, they looked at their experiences as daughter, mother, and now adult daughter-mother with fresh eyes, and they reached their own new insights which illuminated, comforted, and reassured them.

I always relish the moment when the light would go on in their eyes as they realized that their mother loved them in the best way she knew how and that their efforts as grown women and mothers were a gift they had given their now departed mother.

Having learned from experience how to help these women, I now knew I needed to do the same thing for myself. I tried to begin before my mother passed, by contemplating all that had gone before, what was now happening, and what was to come, so that I would not have to start from scratch after the final event, or wait years, like some of my clients. But as I discovered, such contemplations were by choice before her death. It was a whole new ball game when it was by necessity after her death, just to maintain my equilibrium and be able to go on. I discovered that it was through stories, hearing and telling our stories, that comfort came.

Humble disclaimer

The advice in this book is not a substitute for counseling, group therapy, psychological or psychiatric help, or spiritual or religious guidance. Nor is it a substitute for seeking medical attention for symptoms which may or may not be connected to the stresses associated with losing your mother.

But it is a call to appreciate the momentous impact of a mother on a daughter and the importance of coming to full awareness, in your own good time, of the importance of your mother's life and death in how you feel and behave every day, towards your children, other loved ones, and the world at large.

The benefits of acknowledging and dealing with the power of this experience are many. You will experience them all, hopefully, as you read through the stories in this book. I want to spell them out here, so that alternatives which are far less rewarding will lose their appeal.

Some comfort and reassurance

Here are some of benefits you can look forward to as you hear the stories in *Mother Losing Mothers*:

- Increased emotional strength
- An end to feeling alone and a greater sense of community
- New physical strength
- The power to let little things go
- A stronger sense of priorities
- A willingness to tackle spiritual matters
- A new interest in making wise lifestyle choices
- More patience with others
- Added appreciation of others
- A no-nonsense approach to work situations
- New confidence in your feelings, your timing, your power
- Greater tolerance for absurdity
- Greater respect for the elderly
- Added commitment to charitable causes
- A renewed passion for making a better life for your kids
- Impatience with falsehood
- A stronger sense of the infinite or the divine
- A clearer sense of your value to others
- A dependable resilience to new challenges
- A deeper sense of gratitude
- A growing sense of wholeness and integrity
- Renewed hope
- More comfort with uncomfortable feelings
- A delight in little things

- A desire to have fun and celebrate life

These things might happen anyhow, over time, without sharing with anyone. But in my experience, it takes a lot longer and may never happen without some sharing. We are by nature social creatures, with a unique capacity to communicate, learn, remember, and project. We are meant to help each other by sharing. Likewise, all the world's spiritual traditions instruct us that God often works through the works of the people around us. So whether it is nature's plan or the divine plan, we have each other for our help.

So to speed up the process, to give you hope that you can get through it, that it will get better, and to help us along the way, take advantage of the help in *Mothers Losing Mothers* and rely on the stories of these powerful and caring women to let you know that you are not alone, that you are not meant to be in pain indefinitely, and that with your attention and patience these trials will transition to transformation and triumph.

In addition to the transformational benefits which can come from sharing stories with women going through similar life passages, there are some major challenges you will be putting behind you as you move forward through the first year or so after your mother's passing.

You may want to ask, how long will it take to ease the pain, to feel normal again? The first year is generally the most difficult, so keep in mind that it does get better. Meanwhile, you will come to realize that you can expect that there will be a new normal, but it will feel even better than the old one. The stories here are all from women in their first year after the deaths of their mothers, since these are the stories I found most helpful when I was going through my first year.

Progress to expect in the first year or so

If you let your healing and recovery process happen, giving it the energy and attention it deserves, your efforts now will definitely make later years easier. Here are some of the tasks and

challenges which you can look forward to getting past in this first
year:

- Sorting out or at least finding a path to resolving
  legal issues
- Changing over names to accounts, car, home,
  possessions
- Carrying out distributions according to your mother's
  will
- Episodes of wailing, crying, and whimpering
- Tossing and turning in bed
- Unpredictable tears in the eyes at the smallest hint of
  a memory of your mother
- A certain feeling of deadness inside
- Not knowing what to say when folks say they are
  sorry
- Feeling that everything you regularly do each day has
  little meaning
- Feeling overambitious that everything you do must
  get done now
- Eating or not eating, bigger appetite or no appetite
- Wishing you were a drinker
- Replaying over and over again the last days
- Analyzing and reanalyzing your words and
  conversations in the final months
- Making excuses for not being up to par
- Wondering why God has forsaken you
- Feeling impatient with the minor concerns and
  requests of others
- Feeling distracted among friends or family
- Wanting to stop the world and get off
- Making all the funeral decisions, invitations, and
  announcements
- Thanking all those who expressed their sympathy
- Feeling sad, empty, let down, abandoned, rudderless

- Organizing or at least deciding what to do with memorabilia and family treasures
- Feeling you have to stay strong for your children and family

There is a lull after about six weeks, when all the relatives and friends have said their piece and the flowers and cards have faded and no one seems to know you are still in pain. Then the process of healing for which this book is designed can begin or not. If like so many American women have been taught to do, even in our generation, we put others first, try to please them, and judge ourselves by their expectations, or we try to be strong and tough it out, we may not spend the time and energy we need to get through this lull period and begin our healing process.

Give yourself a break. Even just the mechanics of losing your mother, making decisions about the physical remnants of her life, will take a year. Tell your loved ones and friends that you need to stop, regroup, do what needs to be done for you, even if you don't have any idea what that is. If you ask, they will try to understand and to give you the space you need.

How to maximize your benefits

To get the most benefit while you are turning the pages of *Mothers Losing Mothers,* here are some suggestions:

- Take notice of what feelings you feel and greet them with appreciation and acceptance. Let them be.
- As you hear the stories of these women and mothers like you and me who have suffered the loss of their mothers, absorb the gifts they are giving by letting your heart resonate with their feelings and impressions.
- When you reread any part of *Mothers Losing Mothers*, notice how your feelings have changed since the previous reading.
- Experience the ideas and information at your own pace without forcing anything.

- Remember that your own responses are the most valid and valuable ones for you and deserve your attention and acknowledgment.
- Skip around in the book if something grabs your attention.
- Share *Mothers Losing Mothers* with a friend or loved one.
- Make a list of the people in your life with whom you would be comfortable and gratified to share your story.
- Begin to write and tell your own story about losing the mother you loved.

I invite you to trust your own process as you listen to the stories in *Mothers Losing Mothers,* noticing the tenderness, humor, love, caring, and truthfulness of each, and allowing the unique wisdom of each to help move you from a profoundly tragic moment in your life to a triumphant affirmation of your mother's life and your own.

In the career of female fame, there are few prizes to be attained which can vie with the obscure state of a beloved wife, or a happy mother.
JANE PORTER

CHAPTER 2

MY STORY: FRIENDLY DRAGONS

I wanted my mother to live until at least 90. I had saved a birthday card for her for her hundredth birthday, but she died when she was exactly 83 and a half, August 9, 2009. I had three aunts who lived past 90 and an uncle who lived to a hundred, all with all their faculties functional, so that was my hope. But she lived longer than either of her parents, who had died in their 70s. So I was happy for that.

I did everything I could think of to encourage her to live a healthy lifestyle and to enjoy her favorite activities. But in the final year or so, I knew things were getting harder for her physically, and in hindsight I know she was seeing the end approaching. I knew it was coming of course eventually, but I also had my own denial mentality going on, having seen her pull through other challenges a number of times. Then in the hospital, when the last test was not helpful and the hospice specialists told their version of what was going on, I realized that all my mental preparation was worth very little.

I grew up imagining the fantasy castles I saw in Disney cartoon films, as well as the more somber ones I had seen perched eerily overlooking the Rhine River where the Brothers Grimm wove their tales. The fairytale heroines who lived in castles were girls whose mothers weren't there. Sometimes as a child I wished I could have their kinds of adventures, always with a happy ending of course. But I was happy to be safely with a mother who cared about me. If these heroines had had a mother like I did, I realized as I got older, they never would have had all their life-threatening adventures.

There are other kinds of castles I think of too. There are the stern Norman-type castles with their fortified keeps which dot the mounds of old England, and there are the delicate chateaux of Renaissance France. Then there are American castle-like structures, like Houston Hall, which stands at the center of the University of Pennsylvania's campus in Philadelphia and was the first Student Union in the United States when it was built in 1896.

My mother and father used to meet after their college classes in Houston Hall in the 1940s. My mother's sister had married my father's brother and they quickly became inseparable. They eloped as soon as news of the end of World War II was announced, when they were just 19. Mother used to tell me how they shared a passion for Spanish, for ancient pre-Columbian cultures, and for travel. They wrote poetry to each other, poems I now have. On Fridays, they would go to downtown Philadelphia and take in a movie and then go dancing.

My husband and I first met in that same Houston Hall twenty years later, when we were both Penn students and a mutual friend introduced us. But when a few years later I told my mother I was in love with him, she said, with a straight face, "But you're only 19. I was much older at 19 than you are."

Mothers are complex beings, but they mean the world to us and have a profound effect on who we are. The sadness and emptiness they leave behind when they depart this life is complex and often overpowering. For me the vision of an empty castle put a name on how I felt.

When the vision of the empty castle flashed into my mind, a flood of tears filled my eyes and I couldn't stop crying. It was like the dam had broken. For so many months my eyes would tear up at the most unexpected moments when I was reminded profoundly or superficially of my mother and all she represented for me. But this time was different. I felt a relief, because I finally knew how I felt. It was as if I had awakened from a deep sleep of pleasant dreaming in a grand castle, like an honored guest or even a princess, and had discovered all at once that the royals, their staff, and all their belongings had suddenly vanished. They had all disappeared, like Sleeping Beauty's family, who went to sleep for a hundred years.

For me, that magnificent edifice was still there but the life of it was gone. That edifice would eventually be broken up, like a giant corporation being divested and dispersed into many little companies. My sister and I would have to sell, give away, and divide up all the bits and pieces and sell our mother's beloved home. Many different categories of things had to be dealt with. And the intangible feelings and memories attached to every one of these things were at times overwhelming. It was as if an empty castle was suddenly given to me to dispose of when all I wanted was the royal family to come back. My feelings of confusion and aloneness were almost unbearable.

My mother died from various complications of age and the standard medical treatment for what was diagnosed as congestive heart failure. I have mixed feelings about talking about it, because I think there is more that could have been done, or actually less, and also I prefer not to dwell on sad events. I'd rather talk about happy ones. She was the same way.

My father had died 24 years before. My mother several years later met a wonderful man very much like my father and 10 years younger than she was, who stayed with her and loved her until the end. My mother was 83 and was in good mental and physical health until about a year before her death. She was a passionate traveler and had spent a month cruising the South Seas just six months before her death and a week in Ireland just two months before her death. She was in pain and discomfort in the final months, but was mentally clear and very aware. She was trying desperately to stay alive but slowly realized the end was coming.

I have relied on my sister the most of all people during this time. We were in the hospital with mother every day in the last couple of weeks, comforting each other in the evenings. I also relied on my husband, who was very understanding and saw that we needed our quiet time and an occasional glass of wine, and time to talk and reminisce, review doctors' explanations, and search the Web for ideas.

I had a lot of responsibilities upon her death. I was the child who lived closest and she had come to rely on me to consult about services and contractors, to help out when her paperwork seemed overwhelming, to watch the house when she went traveling with her life partner, and just to have a good time over Friday lunch.

Her life partner Don was stunned that she was on her way to leaving him and he couldn't do much. My sister lived four hours away but shared mightily in the responsibility. She left her family repeatedly for the better part of many weeks to be with our mother during those last months. She and I took on helping our mother with all the medical decisions and then later making all the funeral arrangements and then doing all that needed to be done to settle her estate. My mother did not want our brother involved because they had had a major falling out when he challenged her in court over her wishes regarding family property in her trust, and we respected her wishes.

The responsibilities I took on before and after her death were overall a plus. I really felt that I had a chance to do what she wanted me to do regarding the sum of her life, and that made me feel good. Knowing I could continue to help her even when she was gone was a good feeling. As a family therapist, though, I knew I had to take time to let the emotional and spiritual things happen as I went along. Some moments it all seemed totally overwhelming. Sometimes my sister and I would have a meltdown at the same time. We would hug each other in recognition. Sometimes it occurred for us at different times and we could console each other. Either way it helped to have each other.

We were staying each day with our mother in the hospital, and then we would leave after her dinner and return to my house for some relaxation, talk, and dinner. It was August, so sometimes we took a swim and then watched a movie to let our minds take a break. Then, the last evening before she died, she had been put on hospice care about two days before and we knew the end was close. We debated long whether to try to stay, but it seemed too much for her and for us. So we left. About two hours later a nurse called us to tell us she was gone and we rushed back to the hospital.

It crossed my mind that we should have stayed. I never heard exactly how my mother's last moments had gone. But I remembered hearing on the radio just a few days before then that doctors who specialize in palliative and end-of-life care, as well as most spiritual leaders, are convinced that people choose when to die and who will be there when they do. This convinced me that, knowing Mother, she would want to go quietly without putting us through the immediate shock of her dying right before our eyes. She never wanted to be a burden to anyone and was always helping others, especially older relatives. Also, the hospice service had said she would have to be moved the next morning, and we all knew that that would be impossible for her in the condition she was in.

My last moments with my mother were very sweet. She was on a painkiller, though not enough to interfere with her experience of her passing. She was very quiet, an unusual state for her, because she was always interested in, and eager to comment on whatever was going on around her and for the people she cared about and in the world community. She was quite a conversationalist. But this time, she just repeated, "I love you," and "I love you so much," many times. I responded with the same, trying to be reassuring. I told her she was a wonderful mother and that we would all be all right and that we would take care of each other and that she could do whatever she needed to do for herself.

Though I knew she was not a strong believer in the afterlife, I tried to reassure her that many loved ones had gone before her, her husband, her sisters, and her parents, and that all would be well.

She and I had had many conversations about religion, and my childhood home was filled with discussions of culture, philosophy, anthropology, religion, and the meaning of God for different peoples and times. When I returned to school to study theology and earned my Masters degree, I remember she said, "That's wonderful! I didn't know all those philosophical discussions when you were a child really did sink in!" She was more a humanist than a believer, but she firmly believed that any set of beliefs which helped you to be a better person was a good thing, because being good and kind to each other was what ultimately mattered in life.

Especially because we had always carried on with this kind of dialogue, I was disappointed that she and I never actually discussed her dying or the hereafter when she was actually going through it.

I was relieved to discover in talking with my sister that she did have that conversation with our mother in her last days. That was enough for me. I have always thought it would be meaningful to know when my end was coming and I was content that one of us had had that conversation. It also occurred to me that because I had been so on-the-scene in the last couple of years working to keep her healthy with advice about hydration, breathing, nutrition, exercise, and relaxation – she was always moving a mile a minute caring for pets, plants, garden, house, travel plans, and loved ones – she just didn't want to have that conversation with me.

It helped me feel complete that she knew I wanted her to live much longer. Perhaps she didn't want to disappoint me! It was a relief that my sister also was a great support for her, always encouraging her healthy habits. We felt we had extended her life by years, and she often had thanked us for that before her final illness.

She was the last of her immediate generation except for my father's sister, who passed on as *Mothers Losing Mothers* was going to press. Mother was the youngest of three sisters and survived them both as well as their husbands. My father's brother also had already died. I believe she survived so well because of her fantastic enjoyment of life. She filled every day with activity and was interested in all matters, ranging from world affairs to the brilliant streak of white she was able to cultivate in the leaves of one of her favorite plants. Though she had been a heavy drinker for decades, she let up when her doctor told her she had to, and she paid great attention to information about how to increase health and longevity.

My husband's parents were still living when she died, so my children still had two grandparents. But with me now being the oldest of my immediate childhood family, it does feel different. I think I notice more than I did before her death that I am really some kind of combination of all those who have gone before, especially of my mother's parents, with whom I was very close in my childhood.

I think I am more aware now about how short life is, even if you live past 80. My mother often said that she and my father were married 40 years and that it seemed to her like the blink of an eye. And then she marveled at her 22 years with her new love Don, and she loved to say, "Haven't I had a wonderful life?"

I think the biggest lesson I have learned from looking at the span of my mother's life is that there is no point dwelling on any bad experiences. She certainly had some major challenges but she always focused on and remembered and reminded herself often of the good experiences. While I already tended to focus only on the good, I also saw in her life how to focus only on the positive side of life.

I also feel even more poignantly that your family and how you give to your family are all that really matters. Jackie Kennedy Onassis said once that if you didn't do well by your children then you hadn't really succeeded in life.

I feel more empowered today since my mother's death. It was empowering to feel that I had really been able to help her and see her through to the last. I feel I earned her respect and exerted all my power, skills, and love to her benefit. And that makes me feel powerful. I also feel some relief now, since I do not have so much responsibility in looking after her needs and can really focus more on my own life and family.

I am not prone to depression or muting my feelings. As a family therapist, I know that does no good and I'm not inclined that way temperamentally anyhow. My feelings about losing my mother come and go, and sometimes they are very intense and sometimes they are just a little twinge. They usually come at quite unexpected moments – a word from someone, a smell, a whiff of breeze that reminds me of my childhood, a comment from a store clerk that reminds me of shopping with my mother.

I also keep keepsakes around so that I will have little opportunities to be reminded in more controllable environments, so that I can let my mind do what it must to move forward in spite of my pain. I have a silly photo on my work table, for example, which a friend sent me of my mother and me at a Halloween party and I'm in Mickey Mouse ears. We are both smiling and hugging and it makes me smile when I see it. It also inspires me to keep writing this book because I know she would appreciate it.

Mother loved my writing and really delighted in seeing me on TV talk shows. She always said I should have my own show. Maybe I will some day. She would be excited that I now have my own weekly radio show, on the Web, no less. She would chuckle that it is called *Family First*, since it was her suggestion that I do a history paper on the American family for a fifth grade history class which started it all for me. It was that research plus our many family trips abroad and the cultural education which that travel gave me, which started me on my life mission to make the world a better place by helping people to create happy healthy families and to raise healthy happy children.

Mother was always into learning, reading, traveling, and watching the History and Discovery channels. She even took computer lessons, but never quite took to it.

When I am taken by surprise by a twinge of remembrance I often tear up, but I think that now these days, it's not enough for others to notice. At least I knew to expect these moments, because I went through the same thing after my father died at age 59. Even still, once in a while, I catch a glimpse of a white-haired man from the back, and on seeing a particular curve of the neck I will have an instant recollection of my father and get moisture in the eyes. Twenty five years later. I know the same will be true with my mother.

I think a profound sadness is my primary feeling. I just miss her. I miss her calling me to tell me that there is a show on PBS about Egypt which is showing the temple right where we were when I was 15. Or there is a film about Petra showing exactly where she was, "just last year!"

I miss her laughter. I miss her little red SUV that she hauled her gardening supplies in every spring. I miss the tours she would take me on around her property to show me the newest arrangement of stepping stones or new dragon ornaments in the gardens. I miss her excitement when she told me about the next trip abroad she was planning and what a great deal she got on the cruise ticket because she was such a loyal customer. I miss her insightful questions and comments about world affairs. I miss her every day. I didn't ever talk to her every day, but I always just knew she was there.

It is really different just knowing that she is not there. I always tell my clients not to worry if their kids don't seem to communicate much. Children tend to assume that their parent is always there, a given in their lives. It's a natural assumption. But now for me, a part of the family equation has been dropped out, at least in the physical universe.

I don't feel any guilt, once I worked through not being there when she died.

I feel a huge amount of appreciation for my mother in my life. We had some tough times between us, but she made me who I am and I am grateful. And I am really glad she came to appreciate me for who I am.

Nostalgia is big with me. I love remembering cool stuff, little and big things we shared in our lives. We were privileged to live in a lovely home as children and to take fantastical trips in the summers. There were serious stresses in the home at times, but all in all there were thousands of wonderful things in my young life and in our later years when my mother and I got to know each other again as woman to woman, and mother to mother.

There was much warmth between us, more in the later years than earlier. I think as my mother gained confidence in her own strength and power, she became more overt with her affection. Also there was a difference in the generations. Mine was the flower power, make love not war generation. My parents were open with their affection for each other but more guarded with expressing their affection for us kids. Instead they showed it by being present with us, spending time with us, taking us with them around the world.

Sometimes I feel overwhelmed with the blessing it is to be able to love so much, for both my mother and me. My parents were adamant that love ran the world and I believed them and still do.

I think I still have some anger that the doctors didn't let us all know a little sooner that there was nothing more they could do. I wish mother had not gone through that final diagnostic test, since it seemed clear things were not going to get better and the test was a strain on her. But when they suggested she do it, she still had hope and chose to go through with it, and our hope was bolstered by her passion for life. So it was done.

I have no regrets except for my mother's pain in the last days. I know she wanted to stick around. Her life partner had retired just a year and a half before her death, and she so wanted to take some more long trips with him. I'm glad she was able to enjoy the month cruising to Australia with him six months before she died.

I felt relieved that her final illness was not longer. I know she wanted to go out with her boots on, so to speak, still functioning actively in the lovely home she had created after she sold our childhood home when our father died. And she did accomplish that.

There is a fullness I think in knowing that she was happy with her life and happy with herself and content that we would all be okay. But there is no denying the enormous feeling of emptiness now that she is not here. I find the best way to think about it is to fill that gap with my love for everyone around me who is here.

I have huge admiration for my mother and I think it is still growing. She lived in a time of great difficulty, growing up during the Great Depression and the Second World War, then the Cold War and times of great change. She was able to survive and thrive through it all.

I still feel some stress around my boxes of records and memorabilia from my mother's home. She kept everything. Like so many who lived through the Depression, she stocked up on supplies, and she kept all records and keepsakes meticulously. My sister and I split up all the photos and records between us, but still we each have many boxes. I find if I trust myself to make regular progress with these things, they do move towards resolution, getting sorted out and finding new homes with me or other relatives.

Mother had known folks who lost their homes and all their valuables, and she was grateful for all that she had. For just a few examples, she had letters from the 1910s between her grandfather and her mother when he was traveling in China before the revolution there, and she had her mother's collection of postcards from her trip to Egypt in the 1920s. She also had every letter she and my father wrote back and forth when they were dating and when he was in the navy during the Korean War. And they wrote several times a day. I suppose it was a lot like texting today between sweethearts!

My mother didn't like confusion. I have little tolerance for it either. That's why I make so many lists. And I expect people to know what they want and ask for it. If something is confusing to me, then I rely on my faith that it must not be the time to make a choice yet, and I set it aside until the answer is clear.

I remember what Albert Einstein said, that to solve a problem you must explore all angles and then set it aside and do something else, like sleep on it. Then a new way to solve it will come to you. Also, he said, you never solve a problem by thinking about it at the same level at which it arose. So if there is confusion, I take a good hard look at the problem and then figure out how any decision can be postponed until a more relaxed and broader perspective can make the solution clear.

Fear can come and go for me. Fear about what my mother must be going through in leaving the life she loved was the worst part of the whole process for me, because there was nothing I could do to lighten her load. I guess afterwards I was also fearful about getting everything done as she wished with her belongings and memorabilia, since she had worked so hard to create them and to keep them safe, and she had taken great pains to make sure we could handle her estate with a minimum of hassle and delay. We were pleased we were able to do it as she had directed in good time.

But I don't dwell in fear for two reasons. I knew we were doing everything we could to have things come out right, before and after her death. And I have learned that courage is fear that has said its prayers. I decided long ago that fear attracts the thing you fear, just like an angry dog senses fear in its prey. So I make it a habit to use some of my quiet hours to contemplate what I might be afraid of and then to let it go. My spiritual practice helps a lot here.

I felt a lot of urgency in being there for my mother in every way in her last couple of years and the final few months. I also felt great urgency to get her affairs settled quickly because that is what she wanted. The urgency prevented us from prolonging the procedure and I am grateful for that, since I have heard of families wrestling with an estate for years, and indeed that is what happened when my father died.

I certainly felt overwhelmed for that year surrounding my mother's death, six months before and six months after. My career was on hold and my family relationships and homemaking responsibilities were minimally attended to. Thankfully my son and daughter were grown up and needed little attention from me. I am so grateful that my family understood my need to be there for my mother.

My financial life suffered greatly but I was just able to pull through. Then my mother's estate helped me get back moving forward again. I am thankful my mother was so careful with her funds and so generous towards her family.

Sometimes I still feel emotionally overwhelmed. I am in awe that humans are capable of so much feeling. Love for a mother and a father passed, love for spouse, love for children, grandchildren, and then the sun and the moon and the stars and everyone under them! It is truly a miracle. Sometimes I feel I will just burst.

It makes me think of a picture I have of my mother on her last Easter Day, sitting with her life companion Don on one side and my son and his son – her grandson and great-grandson – on her other side. She so enjoyed seeing her great-grandson and smiled so much that day. Even though it had been a long time since she had held a two-year-old on her lap and she seemed not quite sure of herself, I believe she felt that same sense of bursting with love that day.

I believe a sense of overwhelm and a feeling of being alone are the most distinct feelings I have experienced, along with the sadness. She just isn't there anymore. Her spirit, presence, energy, love, must be integrated into who I am now. I must find them within me. That can be difficult and lonely work, but it is well worth the trouble. I fill the loneliness by feeling love for all those who are still with me. It's like one of my theology professors pointed out: according to the writings of the New Testament on the teachings of Jesus, the best way to love God is to love your fellow humans and all of God's creation. Likewise, the best way to heal from the loneliness of not having my mother here is to love those she loved.

There is a peace about this process for me. I knew my mother well and I watched the whole span of her life from when she was 23 and I was two, just old enough to remember a bit, to when she passed on at 83. That vision of a life gives me a sense of peace, that life is beautiful and meant to be enjoyed, as she enjoyed it. We are here but for a short time and it is love in the present that matters. That is a great source of peace for me.

I know from my spiritual work and my work counseling families for over 25 years that feelings result from our way of looking at the world. Certainly we have basic feelings that are there from our early evolutionary days just to help us survive, like hunger, thirst, defense of self and family, the desire for human touch, the urge to reproduce, and the pull to nurture babies. But the emotions most of us deal with every day are not these basic mammalian urges but rather feelings that depend on our previous perceptions and experiences. So I believe if you have a feeling you don't like, you can change it by accepting it without judgment and finding what assumptions about your world it is based upon. When you have done that, you can then reexamine those assumptions and draw different conclusions and the feeling will resolve itself.

So this is the process I use when I don't like my feelings. For example, when I feel sad, I take a look at my perception that I have had a great loss. By thinking through how much my mother gave of herself to me and how much I enjoyed giving her my love and attention, my feeling of sadness evolves into a feeling of gratitude.

There weren't any surprises in my children's reactions to their grandmother's death. They were very appreciative of who their grandmother was and how much she cared about them. They were sad and understanding of what I was experiencing, but they seemed to take it in stride. I remember when my grandmother died, with whom I had been very close. I was very sad, but I did not ask myself the kinds of questions I ask myself now. As a child it seems so natural that old folks die away. Now I realize of course that my grandmother wasn't really that old, just still in her 70s.

My son and daughter were both in their early thirties when their grandmother died. They had been closest to her when we shared holidays and birthdays and made family visits from time to time, when she loved to prepare a dinner for us all.

As a grandmother to my children, I remember she loved watching them grow up. But she was proud of being a non-interfering grandparent. My children always smiled at her and answered her questions delightedly and respectfully and she loved that. She was a great linguist and communicator and appreciated they were so courteous and well-spoken.

She surprised me when I told her we were going to educate them at home, because I thought she would be shocked, since education was held in such high esteem in my family. But she quickly explained that her cousin who became an editor at *Time* magazine had been home-educated and that another cousin had educated her children on a sailboat while cruising the Mediterranean from port to port. She found it intriguing, and I explained how I felt that my most important education came not from school but from the month we spent each summer as a family touring the world.

It meant a lot to me that she appreciated all the effort we were putting into raising our children. Looking back, I think she felt validated about her own parenting, since she had given up her studies towards her doctorate in sociology to devote her time to her children. She said she never regretted her decision. Having worked with juvenile delinquents when earning her Masters, she felt that the only real solution to helping kids not to go bad was to support healthy families, and she was determined to do that herself.

Mother loved having pictures of her children and grandchildren all around her house. I also remember when she came to her great-grandchild's one-year-old birthday party. She was so delighted.

I don't know what my children will ultimately remember best of her. They were happy to keep some keepsakes of hers. She loved dragons and had named both of her homes after dragons: Dragontarn, where we grew up, and Dragontor, where she lived after our father died. Dragontarn was made of stone and was designed by her architect father in the Frank Lloyd Wright style she and my father wanted. She thought of it as her castle. And when people asked her why dragons, she always pointed out that she thought only of friendly dragons. These were the good-luck dragons of Asian tradition, not the nasty dragons in European folklore nor the image of the bad dragon St. George slew.

My son took four of her garden dragons and arranged them on his back lawn around his fire pit. My daughter treasures some wall hangings and jewelry of my mother's. I think they will remember her laughing and chatting at holiday dinners about her travels, the wild birds and raccoons she fed, world issues of the moment, and her delight in her house cats and the occasional wild cat she fed.

Mother always loved her cats. As children we always had at least one cat in the house and often more than one, along with a large dog, a Husky or a Great Pyrenees. We raised several litters of kittens and had lessons in child birth and parenting from our cat families. Mother took great pride in finding good homes for each kitten.

She didn't replace the Husky when the dog died a few years after my father died, but she always kept two cats. During her last years, she had a 20 year old cat which she kept alive way beyond its capacity to care for itself. When she was in the hospital one time during her last year, we could not tend her there and the cat at her house. We convinced her we had to put it down because the veterinarian said it could not be saved and might not live anyhow until she got out of the hospital. She agreed to let her cat pass on. I had to say goodbye to the cat at the vet's office for her. It was a difficult moment. Her life partner Don inherited the second cat. He is a cat lover as well and this cat plus a new one keep him company in his new apartment.

My husband and I have had a cat or two most of our married life and our children also love having a cat or two to share their homes.

My husband was very supportive and willing to listen to whatever I wanted to share about my feelings and about my projects relating to my mother. Though like most men he has a tendency to try to fix things, I was impressed how he listened and supported rather than jumping right in with an explanation or a bit of advice. He knew I had to go at my own pace, and he took on a lot of household responsibilities to give me time both to do what I had to do and also to do nothing when I needed to do that. My husband also helped find a new place for Don to live in, a lovely new retirement community, while my sister and I were working to get my mother's house ready for sale.

My husband lost his mother a year after I lost mine. He had much less to do on the physical end because his father is still living and his sister and brothers all were involved in the various transitions. Also, she had lost much of her short term memory and went rather quickly in the end. He doesn't talk a lot about the experience but when he does, it is with love and appreciation of his mother. I don't think men talk much about when their mother dies, though I think it affects them profoundly just as it does us.

My thoughts about being a mother have not changed a great deal with my mother's passing. I want to stay around as long as possible to enjoy my children, grandchildren, and great-grandchildren as my mother did, but I always wanted that. I think her influence on my attitudes about parenting was already integrated into my being by the time she passed away. Of course as a parenting expert and author, I had already given a great deal of thought to the experience of being a mother. But seeing the full arc of her life as a mother makes me more aware of the extraordinary and ultimate significance of motherhood.

I have believed, and believe even more strongly now, that parenting is the most important job on the planet and that our society doesn't value it enough or let people do enough of it. As a sociologist my mother felt very strongly about that too.

My mother and I did talk about motherhood at different times during my life. In fifth grade when she suggested I do my paper on the history of the American family instead of on some battle or president, I didn't know that there was any other kind of family from the one I knew or that there was such a thing as a "history of the American family." But that project planted some seeds which are still bearing fruit to this day, and even in this book. I remember she loved my first book, *You Can Postpone Anything But Love*, and loved seeing me on television talk shows sharing about how to communicate with your children and help them prosper.

I think I see a bit more of her in my children now when I look at them, especially now that there are lapses of time when I don't see them for weeks or even months. I also feel even more sentimental at times, knowing that they will one day miss me as I miss my mother. But that is a long way away, I hope. I am even more eager to keep myself healthy and strong for the long haul.

The qualities I see in my children which may come from her are a willingness to share their thoughts clearly and passionately and to listen with an open mind to others. They know their own minds and are inquisitive and determined. They are also always active, working on some project or activity which has meaning for them. And they value relationships and try to help others. Plus they are fun, they have a great sense of humor, and they care about the world. These are great qualities they are carrying on.

My mother and I had lunch each Friday for the last couple of years of her life. It started when I decided to interview her with a tape recorder about her life. We did that for about a dozen luncheons and when she said she was finished, we decided to keep up the lunches. It was a great time, because we really got to know each other better just woman to woman.

Over the years she became more comfortable with expressing her affection. Her parents had been quite Victorian, not very expressive of feelings, except to their grandchildren, from which we benefited greatly. There was a great cultural taboo about "spoiling" children with your affection in the early part of the twentieth century. I never bought that and lecture against it. Spoiling only comes from substituting other things in place of daily love and affection, like extra privileges, toys, games, exemptions from a rule or a chore, or some kind of negotiation or capitulation regarding your parental prerogative. Just being there, loving, playing with, and enjoying your children, is never a bad thing.

Mother eventually came to agree with me that showing love and appreciation is never a bad thing, and she loved saying how much she loved and enjoyed her children and grandchildren.

We used to kid about me being the mother now when I gave her nutritional advice. We chatted about all kinds of current events and values and usually agreed about them. She had felt hurt when I didn't take her advice about my husband back when we started dating, because he was older than me and not an oil tycoon, but she eventually realized he was the one for me and came to love and admire him and to appreciate his willingness to help her whenever she wanted.

I still consult her judgment when I am facing a decision. As one of the steps in my process, I ask myself, what would the most evolved version of my parents think is the best choice for me?

The first Christmas after my mother's death was hard because her absence was so hopelessly obvious. Also my sister and I were super busy up until the holidays and had a lot on our minds. Having had a family celebration including my mother and my father, or later with my mother and Don over Thanksgiving and over Christmas every year for decades, the family group seemed suddenly small and quiet. I was grateful that my sister wanted to get together and do things a little differently from the usual for her too. She would often come down and bring her family from Massachusetts or New York to share the family holiday with us and Mother. This time I and my family went to her family.

It helped to celebrate the holiday in a different environment. We shared our precious little memories and toasted our mother. It also felt good to get together with our mother's beloved Don, who enjoys his new retirement community and is starting to travel again.

I make sure there are pictures of my mother and father around, especially at the holidays, and I like hanging a few holiday decorations which I have kept from my own childhood. They remind me to tell my children a few old family stories. My father took a photo of us each year for the family Christmas card and later made an album of them for each of us. I like to share that with family each year.

What reminds me most of my mother in my daily life can be almost anything, like a beautiful day, plants that are thriving (my mother had two green thumbs), chopping eggs or lettuce a certain way, watching international events unfold, or reading about archaeological finds or new discoveries in health or animal behavior. Also various paintings I inherited that she or my father painted. They were both quite talented in oil painting.

The best way I can describe my feelings at such times is wistful. I sense how I miss her, and my father too, and usually a scene flashes across my mind, like my mother in the kitchen, or my father sitting at his easel painting while my mother reads the paper to us kids, or my mother watering plants at the living room windows, or the family unfolding travel brochures together on the dining table to plan our next trip.

It makes me wonder about where all those beautiful scenes and memories of scenes go when we are gone.

My mother's influence had a tremendous impact on my career, or careers, though I didn't know it at the time. After all the travel we did as a family, I was convinced that world peace was possible and I decided to work on diplomatic efforts. I wanted to know international law and work in international business. I decided to study law because I was convinced from my psychology and sociology courses that these fields still had a long way to go to discover how to build healthier families and societies and a happier world.

After law school I took a top job with a leading Philadelphia firm, mainly to prove that I could (this was the early 1970s and I was the first woman ever hired at that firm) and also to learn the real workings of corporate America.

I had accomplished both within the first three years and at that time I realized that the expectations for a young lawyer if she wanted serious advancement was to put in long hours and to place job above family. This I would not do.

My husband and I bought a tumbledown farmhouse in the Adirondack foothills of upstate New York and for the next four years we rebuilt the house with our own hands and with help from the wonderful farmers and homesteaders in the surrounding area. And we tended our organic garden. We also started our family. Our son and daughter were born there in the hardy north, surrounded by nature and farms and family-centered homesteads. It was a priceless experience.

Then we returned to our roots in Pennsylvania when a serious recession hit the country and particularly St. Lawrence County, already the poorest county in New York State. I went to work again but was very picky about whom I left the children with, and after two years I made the same choice as my mother and decided to stay home. But unlike her, I wanted to continue to produce work product that reached beyond the home. I began writing books on family communication and health and taking in family counseling clients.

My mother was delighted with my work but never indicated that she wished she had done more than what she did. There is no question that her time was filled with managing a large home, tending to her children, communicating with distant friends and relatives, entertaining in our home a large number of friends and family from all over the world, and continuing her own exploration of the world.

My mother and I had great times laughing. My favorites from her last few years are two. First, we were having our habitual lunch on Friday. We made egg salad sandwiches every time, since I didn't want her to fix a fancy feast but rather to have time to chat and walk around her property. Egg salad was one of a variety of sandwiches she used to make for us each morning to take to school for lunch. We ate our breakfast cereal around the kitchen table and laughed with her as she made the sandwiches. The egg sandwich was our favorite to take to school each day, so I asked for it when we started our Friday lunches.

We would laugh together when she would say, "You're here already? I've been so busy I haven't even boiled the eggs yet!" Other times she would say, "See? I already boiled the eggs." Her life partner kept cans of salted nuts on the breakfast table. I often nibbled on these while she was doing the finishing touches on the sandwiches. She didn't usually eat the nuts, because she tried to go low on salt. One day I was seated at the table and she was seating herself. I had been enjoying the nuts. I said, "Do you want some nuts?" I knew she did love almonds. She said, "No thanks." Then I said with a twinkle in my eye, "Sometimes you feel like a nut, sometimes you don't." She laughed and laughed. When she had slowed down to a giggle she said, "I love you."

The other great time I think of most often was when she was trying to reorganize her closets to make more room. She found her splendid collection of Chinese brocade silk cocktail and evening dresses which she had had made in Hong Kong when we were there in 1958. The cruise line had told her that if she brought her favorite dresses with her, the Chinese tailors could duplicate them in any materials she chose within 24 hours and have them delivered to the ship before sailing. She did that and ended up with 24 fabulous dresses. I remember sitting in the tailor's salon when I was 10, while the assistants brought out one gorgeous brocade after another for her and my father to choose from. It was a bit boring for us kids, but they were obviously having a glorious time. Later at home, we children would love to hang around when she and our father were dressing for one of those fantastic (they seem so now, for sure) cocktail parties in the late 1950s and early 1960s and she would select one of these luxurious silks, which had cost her about $10 a piece.

Now she wanted my sister and I to try them on and take them home with us, since at 80 she did not have quite the shape she had had in her 30s. We had such a wonderful afternoon, all trying on these gorgeous relics of a bygone era. She laughed and laughed, as she delighted in seeing us wearing them and remarking on how well they fit us. She was literally jumping up and down for joy.

I wish there were more events to wear these dresses to now. They hold so many great memories. For example, my husband and I enjoy ballroom dancing, and I remember so well when my father and mother won dance contests on board ship when she was wearing one of these beautiful gowns. They moved so well together and were obviously having so much fun.

Another great experience I had with my mother a year or so before her death was arranging to have my father's hours and hours of film from family holidays and our many summer travels transferred to DVDs. The woman who did the transfer at Outsource Video took great care to get the order and labels correct, so much so that my mother and I reviewed many of them on video before they were transferred to DVD disks. She got such a kick out of seeing the movies. She remembered so much, even the names of fairytale-like towns in old Germany where we hadn't been in 30 years. And it was so good to catch a glimpse of my father, her husband, though such glimpses were rare since he took all the movies. Again she was jumping for joy.

Remembering the laughter is very comforting. It makes me realize that her spirit is very much a part of my life now. Laughter heals. I realize when I have these memories that her sense of humor and her love of life continue to live in her grandchildren and then her great-grandchildren, even if they won't remember her laugh directly.

I am so happy that she knew her great-grandson. I feel the same satisfaction and fulfillment that I do knowing that my father knew my children, his grandchildren, before he died. They do remember him. Mother's great-grandson was only two when she died, so he may not remember her much in the long run. But she was so delighted to have a great-grandson. I am so glad we could be part of that.

With hindsight, I can now appreciate little signs of urgency that showed in her planning and questions. I now feel for all the thoughts she must have been keeping mostly to herself about her eventual end. She was eager that my sister and I know where everything was, like records and jewelry. We just said, "Never mind that now, that's a long way off." Or we would say, "We'll figure that out later." But she was persistent in reviewing these things with us and felt better when she had done so. I think as a society we don't do nearly enough to allow our elderly to share their personal insights, concerns, and priceless wisdom about life, the wisdom that comes only with age.

As my sister and I sorted through all her things, we found sweet little notes informing us about special items. We discovered her wedding dress at the bottom of an old chest. On top of the dress were a note and a photo from a magazine which was used as the model for the dress, which was handmade for her. It's a dress my mother never wore, because she and my father eloped as soon as the war was over. It was discolored and torn. I spent three weeks restoring it according to directions I found on the Web and now it looks perfect.

Also, next to her lovely engagement ring was a little note saying one of the diamonds was lose and needed fixing. I have since fixed it.

She left in her desk drawer a notice from the memorial ground where she wanted to be buried with our father. When we found it, we felt good that we had done what she wanted. She had also left there in her desk drawer a poem, the one at the end of this book. I believe she had found it helpful in her own family losses and intended it for us when our time came to mourn her.

The activities I find most helpful in getting through this mourning process are those I do with my family, most of all. Also reading uplifting books about family, history, religion, cultural change, and world affairs. Also, looking at photos of my mother and of our family with my mother. My husband has given me one of those digital frames which he programmed with photos of the most recent couple of years. It flashes a new picture every seven seconds, and I enjoy seeing the photos of my mother at holidays or smiling at her great-grandson interspersed with photos of other moments in our life.

Whenever I am in a lovely place like a beach or a mountain scene or seeing a glorious sunrise or sunset, I think about how my mother and all my loved ones would also enjoy it. That's my way of sharing the experience more broadly, on the spiritual plane.

It was very hard for me to drive by her house at first, so I actually avoided it when I could easily have passed by. But now I do enjoy driving by her lovely place.

Certainly gardening reminds me of my mother and gives me good feelings. Also shopping. I often think of the experiences clothes shopping with her when I was a young teen. We were not always in agreement as to what I should be buying! And then I think about shopping with my own daughter. We had many good times too.

I think my understanding and appreciation for my mother's tastes and preferences and mine have shifted a little bit. For example, my mother and father loved playing Polynesian music, sometimes for hours, until we children were tired of it. But now I really enjoy listening to it because of great memories of everyone hanging out together when I was a teenager, swimming or playing ping-pong, still two of my favorite pastimes. I did not take to gardening the way my mother did, but when I am weeding I do find it unusually relaxing, communing with the power of nature, nurturing the desired plants, and indulging warm memories.

When I look in the mirror, I see greater likeness than I had noticed before, like a look of the eyes or a certain curve of the hair line. I also notice some of my word choices remind me of her when they didn't before her death. I think I am kind of looking for her, so I see more of the resemblance.

My mother had a habit of giving constructive criticisms instead of compliments to her children, apparently inherited from her own mother, who was very Victorian in style, although my grandmother was also a bit of a renegade in her time. For example, my grandmother told me how she had once worn a sleeveless bathing suit for a swim competition. When she won, the gossip was that the sleeveless suit had given her an unfair advantage! My grandmother was prone to make little suggestions as to how one could improve oneself. My mother did the same thing. She would say things like, keep your hair off your forehead to look smart, or, put your shoulders back, and so on.

As I was growing up, my grandmother treated her grandchildren very differently. She let us know she thought we were "precious" and perfect. I was glad for the encouragement, but I didn't entirely trust it because it was so different from my mother's comments.

But as a teenager I realized that my mother had never had compliments from her mother when she was a child, though they were very close and mutually admiring later, and that this was why my mother didn't really appreciate how wonderful she was. I decided to make a change there and I started to give compliments to my mother. When I became a mother, I let my kids know how great I felt they were. I think as a result my children didn't have to struggle quite as much as I did to gain confidence in who they were and what they could accomplish.

Since her death, I have awakened with an awareness of my childhood bedroom several times, a very strange thing, since I hadn't done that in over 40 years previously. That has happened less often as the months passed. I believe my brain was trying to interpret all my memories involving my mother, now that the whole story was complete. Otherwise, I have always slept well. I owe that to my mother, who was adamant when we were children that we go to bed at a regular time and get up at a regular time and get enough sleep after plenty of outdoor activity. I have relied ever since on a good night's sleep for daily renewal of body and soul.

In her later years she liked to get up in the middle of the night to watch through her large glass doors the wild raccoons eating. She put snacks out for them every night. Now it was I who was reminding her to be sure to get enough sleep. I knew she was getting a deep rejuvenating sleep, because, like me, she slept on a specially designed magnetic sleep pad from Nikken, Inc. The pad replicates the invigorating energy of the earth, as if you are sleeping outdoors, the way we humans have done for our entire history until we invented concrete, steel, and electricity for our homes. These new substances block much of the energy and relaxation we could be getting every day from being more in touch with the earth. My mother appreciated the idea of health coming from nature.

Another reason she did so well in her life was all the gardening she did outside in nature. She said she loved moving rocks around, as she had done with her uncle Scott Nearing, as a girl.

Just like when my father died, I lost my appetite temporarily with my mother's illness and death. My mother once quipped that losing your husband is a sure way to lose weight. I acquired a gourmet taste on all the cruise ships and taught myself to cook with some culinary flair. I translated this interest into whole, organic foods when I researched what kind of eating would keep me and my family healthy the longest.

I was influenced in this search by my mother's uncle Scott Nearing, who was a pioneer in the back-to-the-land, homesteading, and vegetarian movements starting in the 1930s, all the way through the 1970s. Scott lived to 100 years old. We attended his 100th birthday party in 1983, in Harborside, Maine. He and his wife Helen were authors together of many books on homesteading, economics, world affairs, and maple syrup production, including the most famous, *Living the Good Life*. After Scott's death, Helen wrote a wonderful book called *Loving and Leaving the Good Life,* which Mother treasured.

My mother always admired Scott's dedication to improving the condition of the peoples of the world, and also his insistence on living in harmony with nature. Meanwhile my father was a doctor and maintained that nature knows best and medications should only be used if absolutely necessary. He was shocked by the ever increasing reliance on drugs and chemicals in our society.

I've experienced all the classic stages of mourning. When the moments of despair hit me, they are excruciating. To keep these times short, I remind myself to distinguish between what I can control and what I can't, and I let go of the latter and focus on the former, both in my daily life and when the grand events of life occur. I had absorbed this wisdom from long experience in the Al-Anon Family Groups, to help me deal with my parents' drinking habits. Nevertheless, when I lost my father, I went outside in our backyard at dusk and screamed my head off. It was such a relief and release.

A few days later I asked a minister friend to give me something to hang onto. He said, quoting Psalm 46:10 NIV, "Be still and know that I am God." It was exactly what I needed. It was an instant reminder that a higher power was in control, not me.

When my mother died, that reminder helped but it was not enough. While swimming one morning, one of my favorite times to get in touch with what is going on for me, one of these moments of despair came over me. I used the command from Psalm 46 but it wasn't enough. That comfort seemed dedicated for my father. I needed another to cope with this new loss.

Then it came to me, profoundly. I suppose it came in part from what I had gleaned from my theology and personal growth studies. As I looked into the swirling blue shadows in the pool in front of me and the bright blue sky above me, I received these helpful words: "I am a bit of the divine essence and my purpose here is to enjoy the beauty and glory of the divine creation."

That message continues to sustain me. It reminds me that we are all here for a short time but each has the purpose and the privilege to participate in the divine creation. This message helps to move me to the stage of acceptance and then finally to a celebration of life, partly through the prism of my mother's life.

I relish what I call my smile moments. I smile when I think about my mother telling stories each spring about how cute the baby raccoons were. Or when she fairly skipped down the path to show me her new arrangement of garden ornaments: a family of alligators! Or when she would tell me how fast her day went and she would say to Don when he came home from work, "You're home already?" She would laugh because I had said once that this did not sound very welcoming!

My mother had a moment in the hospital with Don which I felt privileged to overhear. Sitting in a chair by her bedside, he leaned forward and asked her to forgive his impatience in the last little while when he didn't realize she was in pain and reaching her final time. She immediately replied, "Sorry for what? Don't be silly!" He was so sweet with her, and she with him.

Once we knew the end was coming, I told her we would be fine whatever she wanted to do and to do what was best for her. The hospice workers were exemplary and told us this was important to tell her and that she was likely hanging on despite the suffering in hopes of being there for us. I reminded her she would always be with us and in our hearts. In the last days she got very quiet. It seemed she was experiencing her own inner process. Her painkillers were not so strong that she couldn't hear us or communicate. She just didn't need to anymore, I guess.

I was away at college when my mother's mother died. I was still coming home most weekends, so I usually saw her then, and I knew she was becoming weaker. She would say things like, "I have had a wonderful life. It's okay if it's my time. But you must take good care of yourself. You are so precious." I couldn't imagine her being gone. My sister, who was still in school and living at home, has told me that the loss of her mother was extremely hard on our mother. Our father was her best friend but her mother was her next best friend and she respected and admired her deeply. I didn't notice the depth of her mourning as much as my sister did because I wasn't home much, but now I realize that the loss of her mother may have contributed to her feeling overwhelmed when a few years later I was planning my wedding. That meant her mother and her oldest child would both be gone from her life. Loss of our mother affects everyone around us, whether we realize it or not.

Now I know what she was going through. I suspect our emotional process has not been very different, although I was privileged to have my mother some ten years longer than she had hers.

I believe that today's medications cause many of the complications which our older population suffers today, and I watched my mother personally go through this. I wish she could have had an end like her mother and her father, who died at home, with no prolonged hospital stay, with no monitors, beeps, constant rounds of nurses and techs, tests, tubes, food she didn't like, and a rollercoaster of doubt and hope.

It troubles me from time to time that so much of what I know of my mother's rich life and of my own life will be gone forever when I am gone. But then I remember my mantra from the swimming pool, and I realize that the fact that we each experienced them and enjoyed them is enough. Mother loved telling stories from her childhood and seemed to want me to know about them, but I realize now that it was not about me remembering the stories themselves so much as about her sharing her joy about them with me.

She would often quote to me her own father's words, "Remember me is all I ask, and if remembering be a task, forget me."

Mother kept a few very special news clippings and photos under the glass of her desk top and dresser, reminding her of her favorite people and places. I treasure these because she did.

My husband and I have placed a great number of things from my mother's life in our home now. One painting in particular my mother had painted of a secret meeting between two lovers in a misty cave in the time of knights and maidens. It hung in my childhood bedroom and it now hangs in my office. I also cherish a wonderful table I went back and forth about many times, to the point of having my husband and others move it in and out of her house several times. I was afraid it would remind me too much or too often of the myriad of rich events which took place around it, since it was the centerpiece of the great room – what we called the "game room" – when I was growing up. But I am so glad I kept it.

It's an old Victorian table which the restorers called a rare Victorian Gothic style. One day my grandson was playing underneath it, among intricately carved and mammoth legs. Suddenly I remembered playing under it myself at my own grandmother's house. For decades I had remembered playing under a table and watching adults' feet pass by. It was one of my earliest memories. But I couldn't ever remember what table it was.

This was it. What a chuckle I had, and I did my best to share it with my mother in spirit and to tell my children and husband about it.

Certainly it is a bit of a shock to be the oldest living generation. There is a feeling for me that I have arrived, in the sense that my mother left with a good feeling about who I had become. That segment of my life is complete. I already felt grown up and adult and very sure of the paths I have chosen. But I might be a bit more assertive since her passing. I thank her for wafting that bit of new power to me. There is a stronger sense now that I know what I know and I know that I know it. Less in life seems tentative somehow.

My husband says I am more assertive. I have less patience with nonsense and lack of clarity. Luckily he sees it as a good thing. I am also letting my hair fall a bit more over my forehead. I look smart enough.

I did as my mother would have wished and notified all her distant relatives and friends whose addresses we could find, and when I heard back from them I wrote notes thanking them for their expressions of sympathy. It reminded me so much of my mother's determination to teach us to write beautiful thank you notes to my grandparents and aunts and uncles for their Christmas gifts, even if I wasn't that excited about their gifts. It really felt like full circle, and even now brings tears to my eyes.

The most beneficial things people have said to me in sympathy are about how hard it must be or an acknowledgment of how hard it actually is. The latter comes from other women who have already lost their mothers. I notice that it doesn't matter for them in such cases whether it was a year ago or twenty years ago. They still remember how painful it was and offer heartfelt empathy and compassion. These well-wishers are willing to recognize the depth of feeling, the sadness and aloneness, without any mitigation. That's why I am writing this book, to give that recognition to others who have suffered this very poignant loss.

I am big on ceremony. But it needs to be delicate and sensitive, not long and lugubrious. I want ceremony to be more like a spontaneous prayer than a long rehearsed recitation. I do like color, and music, and pageantry. But not necessarily for mourning. I think lighting a candle, gazing at the moon, walking slowly as if in a cloister, preparing a loving family meal, or even rhythmic swimming, serves as my ceremony today. I also feel as if working on my mother's memorabilia is a kind of ceremony for me. And stopping to look at a photo of her from time to time.

My mother wrote a great deal in the first year or two after her husband died, and she would call me in the evening to read her latest poem about her loss, their love, and what they had dreamed and lived together. I hope one day to publish some of these works. She was an avid writer of diaries when she traveled, and it all started when she traveled in Europe with her parents in 1939. She tried to get us to write diaries when we were kids traveling each summer, and we did so for a number of years, but I would have to say, rather half-heartedly. But she could pick up one of her red-bound diaries from twenty years ago, leaf through it, and get all excited again about the experiences she had had. Her mother had collected postcards wherever she had traveled. We were the Kodak generation. I focused on the pictures I took and the albums I filled. Diaries weren't my thing. There is a question of cosmic proportions I think in asking what is to become of all these images in the future? Now they are all being uploaded to the digital cloud. What will be their impact, if any?

I don't spend a lot of time contemplating the afterlife. I cannot know much about it now, nor does anyone else, I think, except for perhaps a privileged few who have come back from death, and I find that today is so rich and full that trying to speculate about what happens next seems far less interesting. I do like to think that my mother is enveloped in light and happiness and has a large grin and persistent laugh now that she knows and understands all. I often feel that both of my parents are reassuring me that my efforts are good and that it's all good and that there is really nothing to trouble myself about, only love remains.

Some are kissing mothers and some are scolding mothers, but it is love just the same, and most mothers kiss and scold together.
    PEARL S. BUCK

CHAPTER 3

WHY YOU AND YOUR GENERATION ARE SHARING A UNIQUE EXPERIENCE

So many women who are mothers themselves and now losing their mothers, feel that they must go it alone and get on with their lives. They are often stunned by the many effects of the event, subtle and not so subtle, and yet they may have nowhere to turn to check that they are not losing it in being so affected.

In this chapter you will find out that you are not alone, because there are millions of American women who are going through this experience of loss, now and in the next few years. Likewise, you will find out why your experience and that of our generation may be unique in history because of the changes in the home and in our society which have changed the way we experience our mothers and the way we experience their deaths.

When my mother died, I felt that I had been through a firestorm and that although I still looked the same and could smile at my friends and go about my business, I was changed. Yet no one could tell. Within the next few weeks I encountered a number of women who told me that their mother had just died too. It was like when you are pregnant and suddenly it seems like every woman you see is pregnant.

We mature women now mothers ourselves and in the process of losing our mothers are not alone. This once in a lifetime human experience is unique to each of us, but there are millions of women all around us who are facing the same event.

Let's look at the numbers for a moment.

Ten million women

There are over 10 million of us American women who are mothers ourselves and are now in the process of losing our own mothers. More mothers are going through this loss than ever before in history. This is because we are the largest generation ever, the famous baby boom generation, born after World War II when our soldier fathers came home from Europe and the Pacific and were desperate to reestablish normal life. They married and quickly had kids. That was us, between 1946 and 1964, 76 million of us, some 38 million of us women.

Around 10% of us 38 million baby boom women have already passed on, but there are still about 34 million of us. About 85% of us became mothers, contrasted to just 80% today. That means there are over 28 million of us living women baby boomers who are mothers, and most of us still have our mothers.

The oldest baby boomers, those born in 1946, turned 65 on January 1, 2011. In an article entitled, "Baby Boomers Approach 65 – Glumly,"[1] the authors summarized, "Every day for the next 19 years, about 10,000 more will cross that threshold. By 2030, when all Baby Boomers will have turned 65, fully 18% of the nation's population will be at least that age," compared to just 13% today. "And one of us is turning 65 every 20 seconds." This means that one of us baby boom women turns 65 about every 40 seconds.

Assuming our mothers to be 20 to 30 years older than we are, they are turning 85 to 95 while we are turning 65. The bulk of baby boomers are in the middle of the generation, born around 1955. These women are in their mid-fifties as we enter the second decade of the 21st century. And as they reach 55, their mothers who are still living are reaching 75 to 85.

---

[1] D'Vera Cohn and Paul Taylor, "Baby Boomers Approach 65 – Glumly," *Pew Social and Demographic Trends*, http://pewsocialtrends.org/2010/12/20/baby-boomers-approach-65-glumly/ (20 December 2010).

So some 34 million women are turning 65 in the 18 years following 2011. And almost 28 million of us have both children and mothers. Unfortunately, just going by life expectancy statistics for our mothers, over half of us will be losing our mothers in the next ten years. That's well over 10 million of us.

My first goal with this book is to let you know that you are not alone, even if the society, the popular press, and even the professionals and those around you don't seem to appreciate what you are going through.

Mothers have been losing mothers since the beginning of humanity, so many may ask, why focus on this normal, natural occurrence? The reason is that our experience is unique in history. We not only talk more about our feelings and social events than ever before, but our relationships are different from any previous generation.

The sandwich generation

We have been hearing a lot about the sandwich generation, those of us who feel the pressure of caring for both our children or grandchildren and our aging parents at the same time. But we don't hear so much about the heartbreak, the overwhelm, and the aloneness, when the caretaking of a parent is over.

Every generation is a sandwich generation, so what's the big deal? And losing your mother in her 70s, 80s, or 90s, is the natural order of things, so who can complain?

For one thing, our generation is getting attention as the sandwich generation because we get attention for all our issues, because we are the biggest consumer generation in history. The marketplace notices what we are up to and how we are different. In an interesting perspective on the public perception of our generation as we reach the age where we are expected to be losing our parents, marketing advisers Matt Thornhill and John Martin, in their book *Boomer Consumer*, have this to say about those of us taking care of aging parents:

"Boomers as caregivers and supervisors of caregivers for their parents are finding themselves in uncharted territory. Despite being at the peak of their careers and earning their highest salary levels, they are wholly unprepared for this role. Most everything encountered at this stage is new and sometimes frightening. But the interesting thing is that those who have been through it are at a different place now than those who haven't. Experience is a great teacher even if a sorrowful one in this case."

Their advice to marketers is this: "Unless you have a product or service specifically related to helping boomers or their elderly parents as part of the care giving life stage, our advice is to steer clear of marketing to this segment. If you do need to target Boomers in this situation, do so carefully and mindful that it is a stress-filled topic." [2]

Marketers appreciate, if only for purposes of business, that this is a very confusing, trying, private, and transformational time. You and I want to do it ourselves, in our own way.

The impact of our generation

In addition to us just getting more attention because we are such a large group, we have also led a revolution in the public discussion of private matters. It was our generation which gave birth to the talk shows, where people in trouble and emotional pain could have fifteen minutes of fame on TV while a guest therapist like me would try to make sense of their predicament so that viewers might benefit by having greater understanding of their plight. I appeared on over 50 such network TV talk shows in their heyday. For society as a whole it may have been a mixed blessing, because awful situations start to seem commonplace. Familiarity breeds contempt. But at the same time previously taboo subjects like alcoholism or sex abuse could now be addressed in the public forum. Our generation brought these issues out of the closet.

Because of this more open discussion, feelings and emotions are more acceptable in everyday encounters. We are more willing to hear each other's stories and to share our sympathy and support. As

---

[2] Matt Thornhill and John Martin, *Boomer Consumer: Ten New Rules for Marketing to America's Largest, Wealthiest and Most Influential Group* (Great Falls, VA: LINX, 2007) pp.180, 174.

with other previously largely private transitions in life, it is appropriate now for grief and loss to be more openly acknowledged and appreciated.

Our unique experience

But there is still another reason to focus on this important stage of our lives. Though mothers have always lost their mothers since the beginning of time and have always considered themselves lucky if their mother lived out a full life and became a grandmother before she died, we are experiencing this transition differently from any generations before because of our unique place in history

Besides being the largest generation of women in our history and the leaders in sharing our feelings openly with others, we are also the first generation of women who truly believed we could have it all and have faced the strains of going for it.

Your experience is not only unique to you but our collective experience is unique in history. We were educated like no generation before. We were given every toy, saw all the possibilities on television, and grew up in a time of plenty.

When our fathers returned from wartime, chose a wife and had us daughters, their wives, our mothers, many of whom had gone to work to help the war effort, returned to the home to make a family and keep a middle class house. The American middle class as we know it today was born with us.

To accommodate our mothers' needs and wants for us their children, our economy underwent an unprecedented consumer revolution, from kitchen appliances to plastic toys, preschools, and station wagons, and later from muscle cars to colleges, IRAs and more.

As young adults, we were responsible for a rich pool of educated labor, a bullish stock market, expanding fashion and entertainment industries, women's rights and civil rights, and eventually new retirement plans and senior communities, still growing.

Unprecedented conditions

Our generation grew up in a period of unprecedented growth and stability. The only dagger hanging over our heads was nuclear annihilation, but even that seemed distant with the cold war remaining cold after the Cuban missile crisis. Our world differed from our mothers' world and any previous time.

This era of growth and stability in which we were raised affected not only politics and the economy but also especially life in the home. Divorce was rare and families watched the Cleaver, Nelson, and Anderson families for entertainment. *Lassie, The Danny Thomas Show, The Donna Reed Show*, and even *Bonanza* had a certain comforting stability about them as the characters went about their adventures. And Disney princesses always ended up in castles with their princes.

When Marlo Thomas' *That Girl* and *The Mary Tyler Moore Show* came along, with women characters securely on their own, the world saw that there was a shift going on, but we young baby boom women were already well on our own way, expecting big things of ourselves, our society, and our world.

Our mothers, from the war generation, were for the most part proud and delighted at the expanded opportunities we their daughters had. We did our best to share our sense of liberty with our mothers and they usually responded with gusto. We wished like no generation before that our mothers could enjoy all that we had.

As mothers ourselves, we have taken it even one step further. We have been able to give our children options our parents never had, especially when you compare our daughters and our mothers. At the same time, many of the values of our mothers' generation seem to have fallen by the wayside, but still we relish the rich options for our children.

We can be happy our mothers could see this expansion for their grandchildren and we can feel content that the circle of life has moved the generations forward in this way. But we must also wonder now whether the unprecedented abundance and prosperity of our time has not put limits on the quality of our children's future. With environmental, economic, technological, and social changes facing our children, our mothers are leaving at a time of huge responsibility for our generation, and we must look to all the strength they gave us to make us equal to the task.

The new look of motherhood: outsourcing parenting

So what do these new changes in lifestyle mean in how you respond to your mother's passing? These new ways of lifestyle mean new ways of experiencing the pain of loss. Most profoundly, these changes mean we have had less time with our mothers compared to earlier days, when mothers and daughters worked side by side in the home. Because of our own busy lifestyles, as our mothers age we must spend more time arranging for care and consulting with doctors and caregivers, than any previous generation. And our lives are more compartmentalized than ever before. The loss of our mothers is a basic life transition, but there is hardly time to acknowledge it in passing, and we can be way worse off for this failure.

Little has been said about the profound lifestyle changes these developments have visited on American families. This silence is at least in part due to the fact that those who might take an interest and be in a position to study the subject are exactly those women who have already thoroughly committed themselves to the new lifestyle. For example, the female sociologists, psychologists, and journalists who are already committed to working outside the home and delegating their parenting and the care of their elders to others are not likely to try to discover all the pros and cons. They are just too close. They have already bought into the pros.

I remember a particular incident when I wrote my first book, about the importance of the parent-child relationship in the early days, months, and years of a child's life, called *You Can Postpone Anything But Love.* I urged parents to fully appreciate their importance in the lives of their children and not to discount the risks and losses that may occur if children are left too much on their own to raise themselves, losses to both the children and the parents, no matter how good the caregivers and schools might be.

I'll never forget a literary agent to whom I had submitted my self-published book. The agent told me that I would have an uphill battle finding a publisher, because all the editors at the leading publishing houses to whom she would submit the book were exactly the young professional mothers who would most likely be disturbed by the message of my book and would prefer not to think about it! I also had a psychiatrist tell me that I was going to make a lot of parents feel guilty.

Nevertheless, eventually I had Simon & Schuster, Bantam, and Warner vying for the rights, because of feedback from bookstore owners who were selling my self-published version and noticing strong positive word-of-mouth. So the word came from the ultimate reader and bypassed the screen of mothers who might be made to feel guilty about leaving their children in order to pursue their careers.

The chemical generation

Not only have we experienced this huge migration of middle-class women into the workforce, the farming out of parenting to schools, daycare, and colleges, and care of our elders to daycare and care-provider institutions, but also we are the chemical generation. We have been more willing to turn our loved ones over to medical and pharmaceutical solutions that any generation in history. This has resulted in prolonged final illnesses which can not only change the financial status of a family but can also be grueling for the dying and their families alike.

We are the chemical generation, raised on the new products developed after the explosion in chemical technologies following World War II. The end of life for most of our parents is today far more medicated and manipulated by chemical efforts to save and prolong life than at any time before. Statistics show that more money is spent on the last year or two of life than on all previous years of life combined.

As an attorney, I understand the drive of physicians to do everything they can think of before declaring a case terminal, but our standards as a society could be adjusted so that extraordinary measures could be resorted to less often when the end is clearly near.

As a doctor's daughter, I also understand the drive of medical researchers to learn from the elderly and dying so that life-extension science can benefit. But this too should have its limits. It would be more valuable to the dying and their families if there were more home care and more emphasis on the process of dying, encouraging and guiding family conversations, and alleviating fear and confusion for the person coming to the end of her life.

I am reminded of movies of matriarchs and patriarchs taking their leave of family in friendly and familiar surroundings with one caring doctor and one caring spiritual guide and loving family around, taking turns in saying good-bye. Is it really so great that we can extend life by six months when it results in a highly medicated, highly mechanized death?

In spite of the lack of studies, books, or headlines about these amazing lifestyle shifts, which have literally driven the U.S. economy for the past 50 years, every mother of our generation has been profoundly affected by them, and the contrast with the family lifestyles our mothers experienced, and in which we grew up, cannot be overstated.

I hope you can appreciate now how significant it is that no generation before us has made this deeply emotional generational transition surrounded by such complexities of time pressure, medical complications, fragmented attention, and societal neglect, added on to the inevitable sadness and grief which the event brings with it intrinsically.

The impact of modern changes to the natural order
By recognizing what might be called modern distortions to patterns of life that have existed for many generations before, you can better understand and have compassion for your own burden of stresses, tough decisions, and uncomfortable feelings which come and go throughout this difficult time. I hope this recognition gives you some comfort, knowing that many of us are facing these new

circumstances and that the best way to survive this passage is to do it together and learn from each other's experience.

A mother is not someone to lean on, but someone to make leaning unnecessary.
DOROTHY CANFIELD FISHER

CHAPTER 4

KIM'S STORY: WILD DUCKS

My mother died August 9, about a year ago, at age 83 and a half exactly. I think my immediate family has been very supportive. Definitely my sister Randy was a great support through this whole process. I think as time wore on though, I noticed that my immediate family couldn't relate to how long the grieving process actually is, because most of them haven't lost anyone and they aren't aware of all the different stages you go through and how all of a sudden you can just burst out crying, even after a year's time. They are very supportive, of course, when that happens, but they say, "Are you all right? What's the matter?" Then I explain why I'm breaking down and they say, "Oh, it's okay, she's in a good place," and "Don't worry," but they're surprised when I have these moments so long afterwards.

There's definitely a void that I think family members don't feel, and they don't sense that you have that void. They don't sense that you have these moments. You could just be standing there looking out the window and suddenly you have a feeling of grief and they don't understand how that could be. They ask, "What happened? What's the matter?" And you say, "I'm thinking about my mother," and they say, "Oh, why?" as though to ask "You're still thinking about it?" I think it is not easy for people to understand if they haven't experienced a serious loss of someone immediate to them. And now that I've lost both parents, my father when I was 28 years old, I do feel an extra burden that my family doesn't feel. No one in my family has this loss. They all still have their parents.

I've gotten the most support from my sister, because she and I are in the same boat and we both have the same losses. So we fully understand each other's place, where we are in our lives and what we have to deal with. It's really comforting to have somebody who I can relate to.

The responsibilities after our mother's death were immense. I look back now at the intensity of those six months and there was almost an urgency to it to push as hard as possible to get it over with. In a way it was cathartic. Our sense of responsibility from the beginning was high, growing up as young children. I had a huge sense of responsibility all the way through. And actually when I was a teenager, I was trying to shed that responsibility, but by the time I was 21 or 22, I couldn't discard it anymore and I was back to being horribly responsible.

When our mother finally passed, there was another change. When she was alive I felt I had a safety net in many ways, somebody to fall back on. If I had any problems, she was there. I just had that false sense of security, so that when she passed, all of a sudden there was an urgency, a fear, got to get these things done, what would she do if she were me, how would she handle this, and feeling I had to do it right. Get it done right, get it done the way she would expect me to do it, and so I felt a burden. I felt that we had to move as quickly as possible just to get the burden off of ourselves to move on.

And up until perhaps a month ago when we finally sold her house, I had a kind of nervousness. It's starting to pass now but it's slow going. I'm starting to breathe, even though there's still residual tension. I don't have any question whether we did do the right thing or how we handled it. My sister and I were a great team to try to resolve all the issues, but we did have the emotional burden. I know for some people it takes three or four years to settle their parents' estates. I didn't want that to happen for us, and I know our mother didn't want that to happen. So I think we managed the responsibilities very well.

About the last day – this is going to be the hard part. I think those last few weeks were very awful for her. For me, her suffering was hard to witness but she remained as strong as she could. She suffered from edema, her exasperation that she didn't understand why this was happening to her, and the elemental fact that she didn't want to die. I still have trouble overcoming that memory because she really didn't want to go. Ten years ago she became very ill and was lying on her bed saying, "I guess I had a good life. I guess it's over." Back then she was resigning herself to the fact that she was passing. But she recovered beautifully. This time last year, on the contrary, she was doing everything she possibly could to get back on her feet and return to her life. She just wanted to live.

It was very difficult to have her saying over and over again with every single breath she took, "I love you." She would just take a breath and say, "I love you," take a breath and say, "I love you." And then at one point she asked, "Am I going to die?" I couldn't answer. Another time she just flat out said, "I'm dying." I winced and dismissed it, saying, "Oh, no you are not, it will be alright." I was so hopeful that she was wrong.

But there was a moment, the day before she died, that I was alone with her in the room and I don't think I even told my sister this yet, but I was on the left side of the bed and she was on the morphine drip and not able to respond. And then for one split second, she suddenly became alert and looked at me with her eyes wide open and I believe she recognized me. I gave her a kiss and then she went right back down under. It was a great moment, but she couldn't speak. She just looked at me with her eyes, so close – it was truly our last goodbye.

And then after that, the difficult part was leaving the next night, her last night. Her nurse had wheeled in the cot for me to stay but after some vacillating, I left with my sister, though I didn't want to leave. I didn't want to leave my mother – what if it was the last time I would see her? But in any case, we left and two hours later it was the end. I think what we did was good, because I found out afterwards that her morphine drip was actually very mild, so that when the hospice care specialist came in and discussed her situation in front of her, she was just too weak to respond, but she probably was able to hear everything we said; she probably was able to hear our reactions. Therefore I'm sure that she was hearing us grieving the last day and when we told her that she should go, that it's okay, you can go now, that's when she started to let go, because she was holding on with such tenacity. Watching her hold on like that was just really difficult for me and I didn't want to part from her.

There was absolutely no doubt in my mind that she waited until we left. She may have even been thinking, "When are they going to leave?" Perhaps she was ready, and was struggling to stay for us at that point. She had stayed until that last day, until we all had again said our goodbyes.

I feel fulfilled in many ways that we were able to be there at her bedside near the end. A few weeks before, she really wanted to try to go home and have hospice care and we succeeded to fulfill that wish. But after a week she knew that she had to go back into the hospital. So I think we followed her along the way she wanted to go, and it was only near the end that we had to convince her that there wasn't going to be any future here on earth, that she had to move on. The stickler for me was that she really wanted another ten years and she couldn't have it.

A funny thing happened with Don, her life partner. He said to me, "Tell her Jesus loves her." I replied, "I think you should tell her that." I stepped back and he went up to her bedside and said, "Jesus loves you." Then he instructed her, "Say 'Jesus loves you.'" It felt awkward, because I knew she was not religious. However she just looked up with this really sad look and she said, "Jesus loves me." Don felt he had done the right thing and I guess maybe she felt she had also.

I felt there must be more the doctors could do. I was bringing my laptop every day and researching her condition, trying to find a solution, some other recourse, perhaps a heart valve repair or replacement. And the one doctor had said, "There's lots of hope, don't worry, she'll be back on her feet in two weeks." And then the next day another physician told me to forget about it, there is no such thing as valve replacement for someone of this age in your mother's condition, and this is it. When I was sitting next to her bed, sitting across from Don, and telling him there must be something else we can do, I know now that she was hearing me, although I didn't know then. I am glad in a way that she was, because she knew that we were doing the best we could to try to help her find any alternative, if there was one on this green earth. She couldn't do it for herself. Although her brain was still very active, she was too weak to think through any options. A week before, she could only ask where her purse was and wanted to keep it close to her. Then it got to the point where she only wanted to know where her spoon was. Her needs were becoming more and more basic. Her world was shrinking.

The pulmonary stress was just beyond belief. Even though the doctors were trying everything, her body as an organism was giving out. In retrospect, I realize her health was failing a year before. She had had a peripheral artery bypass, but despite that she recovered quite well. She kept herself very busy. She loved to work outside, pulling weeds in the garden for two to three hours at a time, and then she would suddenly want to stop, exhausted. She was already quietly suffering and not really willing to admit it.

When we got the call, telling us that she had passed, we went to the hospital to see her. That was so difficult, but at the same time it gave me great comfort, because I felt that her spirit had passed out and that her body was just the shell. It was almost like a cicada shedding its skin. I had gotten a very different reaction when I saw my father after he had passed at age 59 - he looked much more peaceful. She did not, but the difference was that she had suffered near the end. I was pleased to say that I felt that her soul and spirit had gone out of that suffered body. The body itself had been holding her back in a way, containing her. And I was glad to see that she was released from it.

I felt a sudden twinge - oh no, she is gone, I don't have her any more. I now have to be more in tune with *me* having children who are going to have children, that I'm going to be a grandparent and I won't have a parent to help me be a grandparent.

Then slowly, although I don't know if it is confidence, I'm feeling emboldened that no one can tell me what to do - that I'm a full adult as far as that I am the next in line, I am the next generation. Yes, I feel I would say emboldened by being alone now. I feel alone, but not in a bad way - in a good way. I feel wisdom, because, I don't have that sense that I have to look up to my parents. I am the parent. I don't worry about the small stuff. When I see other people having angst over something silly, I just discard it. I'll just walk away. I'm also feeling the need to get things done in an efficient way, because time is running.

My mother lost her older sister Keith and both her parents all within a short period of time. When she lost her sister Keith it was rough, but then when she lost her mother, that was the penultimate. She was grieving for months on end and my father would just go off to bed. She would just stay up for hours wailing and crying. It was really, really sad. And then she recovered one day after this grieving process and suddenly became responsible. She focused on my grandfather. He wanted to be at his home, which they called Opeongo after a favorite place in Canada they used to visit. He would be by himself a lot there, but Mother would be talking to him every day on the phone or she would have him come stay with us, and then we went traveling with him as well. She took care of him all the way through to the end when he had multiple strokes. When he passed, she actually was sad, of course, but it wasn't the same reaction as to the loss of her mother. She had her father resting and sleeping in our house for his final weeks and I think that gave her time to prepare for his passing. A few moments before he passed away, she was at his bedside, and recounted that she sensed he was going. She said she became afraid and left the room. She didn't want to be there when he passed.

My sister and I have spoken often about how sudden feelings come over you when you don't expect them. I have a sense of how I've been reacting. Just two weeks ago, I was looking at the pictures of the interior of her house with all her belongings in it before we cleared out the house for sale, and I told my sister how it just threw me for a loop. I broke down into a ridiculous crying fest and I couldn't contain myself, because it just felt like she was not there but she *was* there – her whole house, this was her. But then I tested myself a couple of days ago, looked at the same pictures, and actually had a comforting feeling, looking at them again in a different light. This is wonderful to have these pictures - they're so nice. And I didn't have the same feeling of compelling loss that I had had when I first looked at them after so long. There are definite stages you experience.

Another time, I was fine, having a nice evening, laughing with my family, and then I went upstairs and I was sending an e-mail to my dearest childhood friend who lives in Bryn Mawr near my mother's house. She was responding to an e-mail I had sent explaining that I was still going through some moodiness and having difficulty moving on, and she had very reassuring responses. I was telling her about my mother's last few days in the hospital and I just broke down. Memories just hit you.

Once I looked up at the big beautiful sky and saw a plane, and I admired the white cloud-like trail behind. It reminded me of when I used to lie on the balcony sunbathing, the balcony that was off of my parents' bedroom in my childhood home looking up, relaxed and secure, watching that white smoke streaking across the blue sky. It actually was a very nice feeling to be struck by that memory. It wasn't despair or grief or sadness. It was actually a warm memory.

I have no remorse of having not said or done all that I could, nor do I look back with great sadness at this point. I know I've gone through the grief of loss and painful feeling that my mother is gone and at this point, I'm starting to feel I'm putting the feelings in their places where they belong. I do have my moments, but in general, the void is starting to fill in with other things. Now when I look at something that reminds me of her, I'm thinking happy thoughts. I'm not feeling empty. It's a beautiful thing. I'm looking at it in a different light. It's sort of like a tree that was cut and then you just let the little bud start coming up and out. Also, the fact that it's spring has affected me in some interesting ways, because of course this is my favorite time of the year, when everything changes and all the trees start to blossom, and it's close to my birthday, and thoughts come back of Bryn Mawr and the wild ducks and geese we had on our pond.

I'm now putting a lot of effort into thinking about a pond of my own on my property, with wild ducks and geese like at our childhood home. I'm going to have, hopefully this year, some chickens and a couple of goats. I'm trying to think about life going on and the good things in life that would go on, instead of pitying myself that she is not here. You don't want to do that. You have to go on. And it's important for everybody else. You don't just sit there grieving all the time. It's just useless.

For a little while, I felt that my ties to Bryn Mawr were gone and I did not feel any need to come back. I tried to mentally say that is over and I was pushing the memories as far away as possible. But given time, I missed going back; it's the springtime in Bryn Mawr that I remember so vividly. And there are lots of thoughts of my friend and me, kicking around in the area of Great Springs, when we used to drive to our friends' houses nearby, and all of the childhood memories flood back of my parents' parties and of that whole area. And even though I didn't like living on the Main Line, the memories of my mother's homes she called Dragontarn and Dragontor are very fond. There are still strong emotional ties, which for me are roots to my parents. These family places created oases that I don't want to forget.

Another old feeling has changed over this last year. I used to resent the fact that no one around me understood my grieving. But now I've gotten past that, and I feel a renewed love for my family and my husband, just the sense of clinging to them more in good ways. I feel that they're there for me, and I'm there for them. It's a renewal in a strange way.

My mother's passing has caused a new appreciation for the people around me. My perceptions of her have evolved too. I had gone through some serious changes with her over the years. We had some intense disagreements. As an outcome of hammering out our issues we became very close at one point when I was about 23 and at that time we had a really good understanding.

It wasn't really until I had my son Rafael when I was 33 that I started to truly appreciate who she was, how she had cared for us, how amazing it was for her to raise three children – because for me raising one was hard. I went on later to remarry and have two stepdaughters Miriam and Claire, so I raised three as well. I used to tell my mother, "I don't know how you did it. Now I really appreciate you." And I actually just point blank told her that she was amazing and I asked her how she had raised us all so well. I learned to understand what I used to interpret as bad temperament. She had a way of dealing with problems: she would just let it out right there and shout about it for an evening and then say, "Okay, I'm done." Then she'd move on to the next thing. I came to understand that this was a self-protective mechanism.

I marveled at her intense interest in world traveling and gardening, and her ability to remember every place she had been and the Latin name of every plant she had grown. She would keep going, in a direction that was positive. Even though she had a lot of negativity in her life, she would analyze it and then let it go and push forward and enjoy life to the fullest.

Near the end of her life she was completely enjoying the beauty of the world around her. She'd look out her window and say, "Oh, my gosh, look at the trees. Aren't they beautiful?" or, "Look at that bird. It's fantastic!" And sometimes it was so annoying when she was talking so much about the wild raccoons she fed, but she just thoroughly loved those little creatures and every second was a joy to her. And this is the way she was all of her life. Life was a joy. The bad in it she would push away. Long ago I thought that she had a flat character, that she was not analyzing things enough, not caring enough. But out of necessity she was just putting things in their proper place, and that's how she was a survivor. She outlived everyone in her family and she was the most beautiful elderly woman, of which she was very proud. What drove her was to be the best she could be all the time and I appreciate that.

She was driven to care for the ones that she knew loved her and who she loved. That is why she and my father worked hard to create an amazing home and collected so many beautiful things from around the world. It wasn't just for themselves, although they enjoyed everything to the fullest. She always told me, "This is for you one day, honey. You're going to have this, you're going to have that." I felt uncomfortable to hear this, but she was setting it up for us and this is what she wanted. I hope I can make my children's future comfortable, too.

Thinking about her generation and ours, I think in her generation she received a mixed message about feminism that she conveyed to me when I was a young woman of age 18, what she considered marrying age. When she was 18 she was quite modern to pursue a PhD in sociology, but then she got married at 19 immediately after the Second World War ended and they started a family soon after. She earned her Masters, but she dropped her plans for the PhD while her husband was in the navy during the Korean War.

She felt a woman should raise a family and that that was most important. And if you didn't have children, then yes, have a career. But if you're going to raise a family, you had better focus on your children and be the mother you can be, and devote every waking second to setting up the nest and making a good education for them.

So at 18 when I didn't want to get married and all I wanted was a career, she hit the roof. She thought this was crazy. And she said plainly that a woman's place was to get married to a rich man and to raise a nice family. He's supposed to be the breadwinner and you raise the children. We had a large fight about that, because I said, "I don't want to do that, I want to work."

I had already gotten a taste of working when I worked in a lab in the summers in Maine, and I thoroughly enjoyed working. I had to hide the fact that I was working from her any other time. I was stuffing envelopes for the Walnut Street Theater in Philadelphia. When I wanted to move down to Washington to try to work in the government, she went ballistic. She said, "You can't do this. You shouldn't do this." It brought up all kinds of negative things for her, possibly because of her sister's experience going to Washington. She didn't want me to get into politics, and she didn't want me to live alone. Maybe it brought up some feelings about her other sister too, moving to New York. It just stirred up demons for her.

I dug my heels in. I'm quite stubborn. Finally I got a good paying job, she was proud of me and she no longer said, "You don't know what you're doing." I was bent on proving that I could be a working woman on my own without family support. But when I moved back to Philadelphia, I moved downtown, not back in with my parents. That is when she had another "relapse" about my independence streak and why wasn't I being what she thought a woman should be, finding a husband and getting married and raising a family? Here I was 24 years old, footloose and fancy free, working in Philadelphia. She just didn't like it. She was worried I wouldn't marry. But we got through it and we started to laugh about it. And she said, "Oh well, you are who you are."

We got along after that much better once she accepted that I wanted a career before I wanted a husband. It was just really strange to her – and scary. She was more scared for me than anything, I think. The way she expressed it to me was with anger, saying, "You're never going to make it," but when I look back on it, she was just trying to say, "I'm scared for you." She was trying to intimidate me to back up and just live what she thought was a comfortable life. She wanted a comfortable life for me. In her mind I had chosen to struggle.

However it was interesting when I got married at age 29. She totally backed off. She was very happy. She wasn't necessarily thrilled with my choice, but he could support me and she felt good,

"I don't have to worry about Kim anymore." When I had my son, she was thrilled. This was finally, "I can stop worrying about Kim."

So there is a very big generational difference. In mine we felt the need to work, be self-sufficient, not have to rely on anyone, and I'm proud of the fact that if I were alone right now, I could survive. I have the skills, I can fall back on anything, I'm resourceful enough. I know I would never be destitute. I don't have to rely on a spouse, on my children, on any strangers or friends. I would prefer to have that feeling than the feeling that she preferred to have, which was generational – that is, you need to have somebody, you need to have a man. You need to have him change your light bulbs, walk you across the street and open the door for you. But I'm sure that that was just social necessity, because she had an independent mind and spirit. She always said she wanted to be a boy and go out on the open seas and travel. Yet I think she was obsessed with the whole idea of her daughters and son growing up properly and meeting "socially acceptable" people to have a comfortable life.

My parents had created a privileged world for us. We had a beautiful private home with an indoor and outdoor swimming pool, a tennis court, a Steinway piano, and a Mercedes Benz. We had the best education, traveled all over the world, and practically had anything we desired. They hosted a magnificent debutante party for my sister, to meet eligible men of course, but when it was my turn to have one, I said no. I didn't want the attention or the expense. But she wanted to give me what she had given my sister. She said, ""You're going to get the debutante party. And you know what? You're going to go to some other parties too." Of course I got hooked once I went to a few. I really loved the international ball and I wanted to go to another one in Vienna, Austria. But she said, "No, no, no. That's enough."

To me at the time this was a surprise. She got me hooked, yet she wanted to keep me close. It's fine to enjoy the world out there, but you have your social structure and it's very important to stay in it. Ultimately she would have loved all of her children to live close to her. In her later years she would always tell me the only problem was I lived too far away from her.

Our family's religious history was altered and I did not know the exact truth until my mother passed away. We found my mother's parents' birth certificates which proved they were Catholic. Even though it hasn't changed my life in any way, it's a shock how they held on to the fact that you cannot admit you are Catholic, and certainly not Irish. My mother's father had changed his surname from McGannon to Grosvenor. The Irish Catholic secret was well protected and my mother didn't even want her own children to know. She focused on our distant French cousins to downplay our Irish side.

I used to think it was more about trying to fit in with society, being more prominent and moving up in society, having a name like Grosvenor instead of McGannon, but it may have been more a result of the times in the U.S. – there were Irish gangs and the Mob and the Irish were considered lower class immigrants. My grandparents were trying to hide the fact of being Irish to protect their family. They wanted the best for their children and to make sure that their children survived as well.

Since my mother's passing, I don't notice my similarities to her any more than I did before, although sometimes I'll see a picture of myself and I'll say, "Oh, I look like my mother." But I definitely notice my moments of anxiety or feeling scattered like she used to and I say, "I'm acting like her, oh no!"

Her criticisms of my life, about the way she wanted me to be, I dealt with long ago. I don't really think about them much any more. I really did wander off on my own long enough that I became my own person and I didn't dwell at all on any of the criticisms. In some ways, I looked at it constructively, because I know she was trying to make us all we could be. So when she was telling me to stand up straight I knew she meant well. When I was young, my mother wouldn't allow me to buy the dress that I wanted to buy. I remember when I got my first pair of glasses; she wouldn't let me buy the horn-rimmed glasses because she said I would look like a secretary. So she picked out clear frames for me, and I did not like them. She said, "You have to wear these. These are perfect."

Those were just her social mores and I have put them in their place. I understand why she was doing it, because finally when I had my own children and they would wear holey pants or some miniskirt I thought was too short, I would critique and comment just like my mother. So I definitely feel that when she was telling me how to smile, not to wink, not to chew gum, she was pointedly trying to get me to be a sophisticated young woman and not just average.

Since my father had passed away, I was very comforted by dreaming about him once in a while, and it was great because he would be visiting me in a park or I would be at Dragontarn out in the game room watching him swim and then he would come out of the pool and he would smile, in my dream. Or I'd be walking in the living room and then he would come up the stairs, and he would always be smiling and hugging me. And it always felt great to see him in the dreams.

After my mother passed away I was getting frustrated, because I didn't see her at all in my dreams and I missed her. Finally she came in my dreams. But it was funny because she was complaining about someone, but also doing that thing she used to do where she'd praise herself saying, "Didn't I do a good job? Wasn't that the right thing to do?" And I was saying, "Yes, yes. Absolutely. It was very, very good," and "Congratulations," and so on. But she was there the way I remember her, a little shorter than me and smiling, with her glasses on. It felt really good to see her. For a little while I was worried, because I felt I have to have dreams of her, this isn't right, I can't just have her in my wakeful moments, but now I know she's there, which means to me that her spirit is around. It's a very nice feeling and it makes me feel like life is coming full circle.

I have some simple things that help me move through the process. Now I am looking up at the sky more often and stopping to appreciate what's around me. Before this I was just focusing on my business, what I had to do and my deskwork. And I am starting to slow down and appreciate what's around me more, because life is ephemeral.

You really have to recapture what you felt as a child. I'm thinking more of my childhood, where I would go outside and play with the animals and sit in the swing for hours, and I never felt like I was wasting my time. I want to get back that simplicity.

As far as dealing with moments of despair over my mother's passing, I distract myself. I'll stop and look at the trees, look at the sky, look at the snow. I'll even sometimes just go up to my room and take a minute just to look at some pictures. I'll just sit and look at some of the black and whites from the boxes of my mother's archives to ground myself, because I love those pictures. It's good to do that. I just say to myself, this is not what she would want. I'll say, you've got to look at the beauty in things, don't look back.

One thing I do have to work on though, and I know she never had this problem, is that I feel guilty if I see other people working or doing things and I'm not doing things. So I don't know where that's coming from or why. My mother never felt guilt about it, but she never did stop. My family tells me I do the same thing. They say, "Why don't you sit down for a minute and relax?" Because I just have this nervous energy like I have no time to waste. My husband Rob will say, "Why don't you take a nap?" because I'll say I'm so tired. I say, "I can't take a nap. I can't do that during the day." We hardly ever saw my mother sit down.

As I now recall, when I would visit her in her late life, she would just be running around, very busy, never sitting, except maybe to sit to look at some slides from her trips or to sit to eat. We would set the table but then we would sit and she insisted on finishing preparation herself, in which she took great pride. And then she would gobble it down and jump up and start cleaning up. And then, she'd be off, "I have to feed the raccoons, I have to call my friend, I have to do the paperwork." I am a lot like that and I hope that I can perhaps temper that a little.

I don't feel any deep mysteries around her passing on, because I've dealt with life and death for a long time. I studied at length in my youth the different states of consciousness, unconsciousness and sleep patterns, and I used to visit cemeteries all the time just for fun, and I was absorbed in books about life and death. I was always trying to examine death and sort out my feelings about it. So when she passed, I was neither shocked nor surprised, nor wondering where she went or what did this mean to me. It actually just fell into place. I knew she was weak and elderly. I knew she lived this full life. However losing her saddened me profoundly. Going to her burial place is uplifting to me. Whenever I go back to Bryn Mawr I visit her grave in the family plot where she is with my father, and I sit there for a little while. So I know that their remains are there and their spirits I feel around me. I put it in its place and accept what it is.

The short poem that was on her card at her burial is a lovely poem and what it says is very true of those loved ones who pass on

– that they are the smell, they're the rain, they're the trees, they're the birds all around.[3] So this is how I accept her passing, and I don't really feel any mystery. I feel that we all go some place afterwards, and hopefully it's a very peaceful place for spirits. The bodies are just remains and they go back into the earth.

My father was a physician and approached life scientifically. Both he and my mother were Darwinists and I too believe in evolution. Although not religious, they were spiritual about nature, which I embraced as well. I think of life clinically. I believe in a purpose for each of our lives. Collectively there is a purpose. Whether we are achieving what we want to achieve in our life or not, that is another question. But my sister had said something enlightening to me: it doesn't really matter whether you are a big achiever or not. The fact that you're alive is the point. Whether you write a book or you receive a Nobel Peace Prize, whether you become president of the United States, or you're a person who is just not a big achiever and made no big impact on society, still you have a right to life and you have the right to be appreciated as a human being. For me that is purpose.

Each person has a role, whatever that is. And maybe we don't know what that is, but we have to accept who we are. That's all that anyone can ask out of life. And in death, the memory is important for the living. You always should remember the good and pass on the legacy. What my sister is doing by producing this book is not only a worthy exploration of mothers' reactions to losing their mothers, but a great tribute to our mother.

My best advice to others in this process is mostly that it's important not to dwell in despair too long, because you have yourself and your own family to care for, and even though grieving is important, you have to grieve, then let go. Talk to other women who have lost their mothers. They say you never do let go entirely. And of course you shouldn't, but it's important to put it in a good place and make it a positive thing, because that's just part of the process. We have to pass on that distinction to our children and theirs. That is a dignified way of living.

When you lose your parents it is a terrible loss. You are alone. They are gone. Your childhood's gone. But despite all that,

---

[3] This poem appears at the end of *Mothers Losing Mothers*.

you must accept it and appreciate who you are now without them. You must keep moving. When you are a mother and you have lost yours, you have only *now* truly stepped into her shoes. I have loved talking about her. She will always be very much in my heart.

Only a mother knows a mother's fondness.
LADY MARY WORTLEY MONTAGU

CHAPTER 5

WHY SOCIETY DOESN'T HEAR YOUR PAIN

You may have experienced directly the neglect which our society is guilty of when it comes to loss of parents. Certainly there are few books about it. There are very few media stories about it. Our society just doesn't do grief unless a major celebrity like Michael Jackson or Elizabeth Taylor dies, or a popular athlete or politician is injured.

As mothers, we are indeed lucky if our mothers precede us in passing into the next world and if they have lived long enough to see us as mothers and to get to know their grandchildren. They have been lucky too, to have the joy of seeing us experience the joys and challenges of motherhood and perhaps even seeing their grandchildren become parents themselves. Then what's the big deal when the generations pass on as nature planned it, our society seems to ask.

On a website for a funeral home I checked recently, there were sections for support in the event of losing different loved ones, including an infant, a child, a grandchild, or a spouse, and on comforting a grieving child, but nothing on losing a parent.

We live today in a highly complex environment with machines and chemicals expected to do all the things we used to do ourselves with the help of nature. But just 50 generations ago, say going back about 1,000 years, there were no engines, electricity, appliances, mass transit, communication technologies, or unnatural chemicals complicating our lives. The very rich could get marble, bronze, and bricks for their homes, but the rest of us were living close to nature. Our mothers were close at hand for advice, support, and help. We often did exactly what our mothers did as we grew up and into motherhood ourselves.

A growing generation gap

There was much less of a generation gap then than there is today because progress was much slower. We didn't have a new form of communication every generation, for example, as we do today. My grandmother marveled at the telephone. Now, it is already replaced by cell phones, texting, and Skyping.

Surely none of us want to go back to those days. Some of us long for the simplicity of those times when we see them in the movies, read about them in a novel, or see their fast disappearing remnants in the pages of *National Geographic*. But we don't want to trade today's conveniences, worldwide distribution networks, global communication, career choices, and public sanitation and safety for those seemingly riskier times.

Now let's go back even further for a moment, say 100 generations, to the time of Christ. There we are in even more primitive surroundings in most of the world. And yet our hearts haven't changed at all since then. One hundred generations is not enough time for any genetic changes to occur which would change how we feel. There was a certain fulfillment we will never know in learning everything you needed for life right at your mother's elbow and having her help you with your new baby and then help you train your youngsters in the ways of the world. And then die quietly in your arms.

Those close interactions and mother to daughter-mother intimacy are lost today. Michael Mendizza, author of *Magical Parent, Magical Child: The Art of Joyful Parenting,* coauthored with Joseph Chilton Pearce, described it this way in his recent blog on the history of parenting: "Children became consumers with disposable incomes and childhood a commodity. To accomplish this, the family bond, influence of parents and extended family in the lives of children, must be neutralized and was."[4]

Robert E. Kay, MD, psychiatrist and natural child-rearing advocate, likes to say that virtually the only children not traumatized by early childhood conventions and interventions today are those raised in the traditional tribes of the Brazilian rainforest, such as were studied by Jean Liedloff and documented in her important book *The Continuum Concept*.[5] Liedloff found that in these traditional settings mothers were appreciated and indulged as they performed their critical role in raising the future generations of their tribe.

Today when our mothers leave us, I suggest that our pain may be even deeper today than it was back then, or at least more confusing, because deep down we must feel the lack of all that we missed.

When we look at the arc of our mother's life, it seems almost unfinished in many cases, because we know they never had all the choices we had in our young lives, choices they had a part in making available to us. At the same time, we see that they had more of certain other riches which we may have missed in our rush to remake our baby boom world.

How many of us really have had a chance or made the opportunity to explore these emotional "Losts and Founds" while our mothers were still alive? Doing so now may help to ease the confusion and burden of loss which so many of us feel.

Society rarely looks back

Meanwhile, the society has never looked back. The economic engine which propels society's progress forward has little interest in noticing what has been lost in moving to the industrialized, information-overloaded world. If the statistics show that your mother lived a good life, well then, that should be enough for you, the collective message says.

---

[4] Michael Mendizza, "A Brief Very Incomplete History of Parenting," *Michael Mendizza's Ideas, Rants & Blog*, http://www.ttfuture.org/blog/2/brief-incomplete-history-parenting (25 February 2012).
[5] Jean Liedloff, *The Continuum Concept: In Search of Happiness Lost* (New York: Perseus Books, 1975).

It is easy to say that a mature woman and mother in her own right can let go of her mother with maturity and awareness and acceptance in relatively short order. But most of us find this is not the case.

Even our spiritual leaders are not always adequate to the task of helping us to navigate these unfamiliar waters. Rarely have they become mothers or grandmothers themselves, most of them still being male. Only now are there outspoken women in the religious, spiritual, new thought, and self-help arenas, who are starting to shout about the critical voice of mothers to help address the challenges we face today.

There have been drastic changes in the role of mothers that society and policy makers would rather not have to consider. Surely millions of women for generations have been balancing work and family for economic reasons. But only with the industrial revolution at the turn of the last century was their work moved out of the home and away from the children for the majority of women. And only after World War II was this pattern adopted as a desirable one rather than one born of necessity, by the upwardly mobile baby boomers, us.

The war years demanded women work in factories while their men were away. When the men returned, babies were born, and it was actually national policy to get the women back into their homes. The "white picket fence" and "chicken in every pot" were the goals. But many of these women saw the opportunity to have their daughters educated and economically independent as adults. From this new vision, our generation of women went to school, got the degrees, and then got jobs.

The impact of economic shifts

As soon as educated middle-class women thought they should get a job, the whole economy shifted with a suddenly larger labor force. Salaries to individuals went down, or at least failed to increase, with the influx of skilled women, quickly turning what was supposed to be an economic plus for the family into an economic necessity. Double the income (or at least 1.7 times the income, since women still earn only 70% of what a man earns for the same work) quickly became a necessity for the middle-class household. Plus there were all the added expenses of daycare, office wardrobes, transportation, and keeping up with the consumer demands created by peer pressure from middle class schools and aggressive advertising.

One time I sat down to do the numbers. I worked out how many hours it took me to do all my home chores, to commute to work, and to be at work. I also figured out what I was earning and what it cost me just to go to work, with daycare arrangements (always in a home, not a formal institution), commuting costs, work wardrobe (suits, stockings, heels, umbrellas), and recreational extras to manage extra stress. It didn't look good. My husband does his share of the home chores, but still I found I was cramming in two 8-hour work days each day. No wonder it felt like something was always being postponed to another day. And the financial payoff wasn't that much. It was an interesting study.

It makes me extremely skeptical whether full-time employees can ever have the relationships they would like to have with their children and spouse. It isn't hard to appreciate why marriages don't last and kids get into trouble these days, when their parents are so overworked between job and home. The idea of life balance is a bit of an unattainable ideal when a mother is working full-time, commuting, and then trying to be a mother and wife and person. I think the full-time employed-outside-the-home mom is still an experiment whose results are dubious at best so far.

For a mother with young children, I think about five hours a day is the limit for work that extends beyond the home. As an expert on family, I advocate working from home if at all possible, to minimize commuting time and dressing for work, and to allow for family needs and to have control over your own daily schedule.

Parenting takes only 20 years in most cases if done well. If you devote that time to parenting, you are preventing problems later. When the kids are on their own, then might be a better time to do whatever else you want.

In addition to mothers becoming employed outside the home, and partly because of this change, we have become much more dependent on professional and institutional health care for young and old, and even our own age group. So many more parents feel they must stay employed if only for employee health benefits.

Combined with the historical developments described in Chapter 3, "Why You and Your Generation Are Sharing a Unique Experience," the now dominant family pattern of both parents being employed outside the home adds one more way in which our experience as mothers now losing our own mothers is unique in the history of the world. We have not had as much of them in our adult years as time-honored patterns of earlier times would dictate.

As a result, the role of our mothers in our lives and ours in theirs has been far different from previous generations, and the impact of their deaths is different as a result.

Despite all these changes which have lessened our time with and dependence on our mothers, it is worse than futile to deny the importance of your mother's life and death to you. Even if we don't see them that often and we are all grown up and have children of our own, their life and the end of their life has an inevitable and profound effect.

Mothers are undervalued

Though our society is currently in a place where mothers are severely undervalued, the mother to daughter-mother relationship is still crucial after all these changes, if not more so. To understand why it is so hard to lose our mother, even when we are "all grown up," mothers ourselves, and fully aware of the events as they are unfolding, we need to take a deeper look at the mother to daughter-mother bond itself. This will help to clarify how important it is for you to ignore the popular failure to recognize the significance of this relationship and recognize how profound it truly is.

As I often say to parents, the parent is the most important influence in a child's life even if it is by his or her absence. And as we grow up and move out, those early lessons from our mothers stick with us. When this first and primary mentor leaves this earth, some of the energy which kept us going may leave too, unless we take the time to renew and reintegrate our lives.

Joseph Chilton Pearce, author of many books including *The Crack in the Cosmic Egg: New Constructs of Mind and Reality* and *Magical Child*, pointed out once again in a recent interview that humans learn primarily from models and that the mother is the first and most essential model for every child. Even her emotions during pregnancy set the stage for a tendency towards defensiveness or openness in the infant, and her example goes on from there. He explains how modern developments have interfered with this foundational relationship, from today's birthing practices, early schooling, reliance on experts, and electronic entertainment, to addressing problems with medications, and so on. He concludes that this disturbance of natural patterns which for millennia have prepared children for adulthood through a close relationship with their mothers is actually putting our species at peril.

Pearce points out that most of us outgrow the need for the primary modeling by our mother, but our learning continues to the extent that we have had the opportunity to absorb from her a strong sense of curiosity, security, and love in the first place.

Naturally then, her death will have predictable impact, especially when we are now experiencing that role of motherhood ourselves. Only you know what that impact is in your case, but it is critical to your future happiness that you take the time and effort to know what that impact is and to let it inform you about your future as a mother, grandmother, wife, woman, and human person.

In her book *Motherless Daughters – The Legacy of Loss*, Hope Edelman explored the tragedy of daughters who lost their mothers while they were still children or young adults. Unfortunately, sometimes we come to appreciate the value of something when we look at what happens when it's missing. Edelman assembled the responses of hundreds of young women who lacked the benefits of having a mother. As she and many of these young women eventually became parents, Edelman concluded that, "Every daughter splits her identification between her mother and her child-self to form a third image of herself as a parent."[6] When the mothering by one's own mother is cut short, you have an empty space where that image of your mother mothering you would have been.

Mothering grows our esteem for our mothers

Only by becoming a mother do we fully appreciate all that our mother went through for us: as newborns, babies, toddlers, school kids, pre-teens, teenagers, the first women to assume we could go to college, the first college-age women to be able to vote, the first women who assumed we wanted careers and then put off family to pursue one, the first women to feel free to divorce if we were unhappy, and the first women to decide en masse that there was no grace in aging.

Only as a mother do you appreciate how her heart ached when we felt sick or how she worried for us when we were scared by an upcoming test, or how she trembled on the night of our first date.

And then there are all the questions which arise when it comes our time to mother. Are we going to do it the same way or differently? Are we going to tell her beforehand, break it to her gently, persuade her it's progress, or hope she doesn't notice or inquire?

And once we are mothers ourselves, do we see things in her words and actions which we didn't see before? Motivations, perceptions, generational assumptions, feelings, which we couldn't appreciate as children but now they make perfect sense? Or not?

Every one of us, I believe, has a different kind of relationship with our mothers. There are too many variables in the life of a family for any two mother to daughter-mother relationships to look the same. Just compare any two sisters who grew up with the same mother and you will find two different relationships. But whether we were close to our mothers as teens or fought all the way, or got great advice about being a new mother or steered clear of whatever

---

[6] Hope Edelman, *Motherless Daughters – The Legacy of Loss* (New York: HarperCollins, 2006) p. 265.

suggestions she might have wanted to give, most of us still arrive at a place with our mothers where we can appreciate her efforts on our behalf. We love her for giving us the best she knew how to give.

The natural role of mothers

It is in our genes to love our mothers and to want to please them. And it's in their genes to love us and care for us as best they can. If it were not implanted in our species genetically, then our species would have died out long ago, because the human baby is about as dependant as any baby animal on earth and for a longer time. In pre-civilization times, in the tribal life of the forest or steppe, if we didn't please our parents or at least the tribal group, or they didn't want to care for us, there would be no next generation. The babies would never live to grow up.

When we leave our mother's body, we enter what I call her castle. She has built a fortified edifice around us in which to keep us safe. Barring extreme poverty, domestic violence, a local war zone, or intractable disease or addictions, our mothers are there for us.

Like the warm, comfortable LeBoyer bath which became popular for many in our generation as a way to ease the transition from the womb to the open air and to welcome the new baby into a world which would meet her needs as they arose, our mothers are programmed by nature to ease the transition from child to adult and to set the tone for who we perceive ourselves to be and who we want to become.

The certainty of having a mother there who cares about you is as reassuring as any castle walls. Her worry when you ventured out was like the moat and the forest around the castle. If you went too far, she would know about it and rein you in. She may not have acted like a queen or treated you like a princess, but you still had a castle to limit the dangers that lurked outside in the larger world.

You knew, whenever you came home, or called home, your mother would be there. Chiding or priding, she would be there.

And it wasn't just her. The castle she had created for you was filled with little and big things that meant something to her. They were a part of who she was. Can any of us picture the mother of our childhood without also remembering the old refrigerator, or maybe her favorite plates, or her favorite plant, or the dress she liked to wear Saturday night or Sunday morning? What was her favorite dish to serve to her friends? What kind of cartoons made her laugh?

Those things populated our childhood lives

They represented in a very real way who our mother was for us. How about the telephone? What color was the phone she liked to use? (Do we have the same relationship with our phone today as our mother did with hers? Do our daughters identify us with our cell phones – or do we just check them often and then get a new one every two years?)

Wherever we first envisioned castles, they were where we wanted to be. Maybe our mothers read to us about princesses in castles, or maybe we watched Disney movies about princesses in castles. Or maybe we just heard about them from friends in school or books about medieval times. Or we saw pictures of them on TV or in *National Geographic,* or we watched gallant knights in chivalric dress fending off a siege or rescuing a princess in the movies.

But wherever we picked up our impressions of castles, they were stable, secure, reliable, forever. Parents are like that. As children we assume they are forever. Nature planned it that way, so that we could have as carefree a childhood as our day and age permitted.

Through our childhood and young adulthood, if we are spared tragedy, we can become very complacent about our mother's continuing presence. Many of us went away to college and maybe didn't speak with our mother for days or weeks at a time. Perhaps we married and lived states away. Perhaps we made the effort to all get together on holidays but didn't think a whole lot about precious moments until we became aware of our mother's declining energy or failing health.

I don't like calling it the caretaking stage. That so undervalues what we are feeling. It is not that we want to take care of our parents. It's that we want more of them. The society amuses itself with the notion that they take care of us and then in the end we take care of them. They enter their second childhood and we become the parent.

But isn't it a whole lot more complex, deep, wonderful, and horrifying than that? We want more of them. We suddenly hear the bell ringing. Recess is over. The hard times are a-coming. We want as much of them as we can get before the final bell tolls. It's not duty. Rather it's love. Yes, they can make it hard, curmudgeonly as they can get, or overly grateful and solicitous, or embarrassed, or doggedly independent. But in the end we love them for it. That's who they are, the mother we love.

We are currently experiencing a trend to discount motherhood as the society attempts to justify the many ways that mothers are pulled away from their families. Don't let this trend to discount motherhood fool you.

Commoditizing motherhood

We have experienced an amazing but rarely remarked upon commoditization of the functions that mothers have fulfilled throughout previous history with their children always close, including infant care, breastfeeding, food preparation, education, family scheduling, manners, sexual mores, religious orientation, nursing through sickness, self-care, work skills, and more. Where our mothers prepared our meals, for example, many of our grandkids expect to eat out of a box while driving in the car.

All these traditional home-based functions are being outsourced, and mothers today who are not expected to perform these functions any more seem to be asking themselves what they are there for except to worry, watch, and encourage. And they wonder why they don't feel more trusting and confident about their children, not realizing that they have been deprived of all these confidence building interactions of earlier generations. This creates a kind of vicious circle, in which motherhood is discounted because it seems almost unnecessary with all the institutional substitutions for mothering.

In addition, there is a worrying trend to medicate our concerns, and to ridicule and even demonize mothers who are devoted to their children, who breastfeed, who supervise homework, who are careful to buy nourishing food, and who are discriminating about what chemicals they allow into their homes. Mothers are being actively discounted. This adds to the tendency of society at large to discount the significance of our own mothers as they pass out of our lives.

Consider the findings of the advocacy group Moms Rising. For example, they have pointed out that, for the same work: "The wage gap between mothers and non-mothers is greater than between women and men — and it's actually getting bigger. Non-mothers earn 10 percent less than their male counterparts; mothers earn 27 percent less; and single mothers earn between 34 percent and 44 percent less."[7] Mothers don't have it easy these days.

Who then will understand how difficult it is to lose your mother when you are a mature, educated, hard-working, responsible mother yourself?

That would be only other mothers who have experienced it themselves and come out the other side stronger, more confident, and more serene. Those are the compassionate voices you are witnessing in this book.

There is nothing wrong with feeling a great hurt

Unfortunately, too many women are convinced that there is something wrong with them when depression and anxiety hit, or they think it just comes with reaching middle age, when in fact, their response is a normal healthy one to a personal loss which will take time and energy to heal even with the best support, like you will find in *Mothers Losing Mothers*.

By acknowledging feelings and helping each other appreciate the shifts at all levels, spiritual, emotional, mental, physical, and social, that the loss of your mother may require of you,

---

[7] "R: Realistic & Fair Wages," *MomsRising.org*, http://www.momsrising.org/page/moms/wages.

you can not only avoid much lingering pain and anxiety but also avoid many mental and physical symptoms of pent-up emotion, avoid dependency on medications for your moods, and even reduce our national health care bill in the process.

So I ask you to trust yourself. If you are hurting, there is a reason. Don't try to self-medicate, get a health practitioner's chemical prescription, or seek to hide in any self-destructive or addictive habits.

Instead, go at your own pace and trust that pace. If you get stuck, review these stories. If you don't get relief and feel you aren't moving forward, consult a professional who has experience helping people to heal their pain rather than medicating it.

Trusting yourself in your mourning process is a very important first step to move on productively with your life after your mother's death. In fact, in interviewing mothers for this book, I have found that this trusting of yourself is a vital attitude at each stage. If you are still trying to react the way others think you should, or the way you think others think you should, you can stop that right now. You are not crazy, overly sentimental, "tied to your mother's apron strings," wallowing in your misery, using loss as an excuse, punishing yourself, or any other concoction that makes you feel bad. Your pain is real and you are meant to feel it. The consequences of succumbing to the fear of feeling the pain are way worse than simply letting your heart take its natural course.

Physical pain is the body's way of telling us that something is wrong and that we must take a break and create the right environment to correct it. It may require better eating, more exercise, more rest, more water, more sunshine, less stress, more prayer, a doctor's intervention, or a vacation. It is the same with mental or emotional pain. It is a signal from the mind to make a change. Take a break and think, feel, express to a caring other, relax, reconsider, meditate, pray, let go.

Don't let our society's public neglect of the seriousness of your experience lead you to neglect your personal needs. Denying pain is a serious mistake. Let it be, accept it, and listen to it. Take the time and energy to find out where it truly comes from and allow it to heal with the tools you will absorb from the stories here in *Mothers Losing Mothers*.

Family faces are magic mirrors. Looking at people who belong to us, we see the past, present, and future.
       GAIL LUMET BUCKLEY

CHAPTER 6

ELAINE'S STORY: BING CHERRIES

My mother passed away July 12th, 2009. It was my mom's sister-in-law's birthday. My own birthday is in the beginning of July, and I remember she was really sick then, and we wanted to take her to our house but we knew we couldn't. So she had a rough day that day, and it was five days later that she passed away. I really didn't want her to pass away on my birthday. I don't know what it is. I think we maybe all feel that way.

I was with her on my birthday. She was in a nursing home out here in Western Pennsylvania, and I spent a lot of time with her every day. I had chosen to retire in December of the year before, which would have been 2008, and my mom and I moved out here from Eastern Pennsylvania.

My son and his wife, pretty much took care of arrangements out here. And Mom and I drove out together on December 23rd, '08. We wanted to be here by Christmas and we made it.

She didn't need any oxygen or anything like that, but the people at the nursing home really felt maybe she needed to be taken in an ambulance, but I said "No, I'm sure she'll be fine," because she could walk with a walker a little bit, and I knew that the new nursing home would have a wheelchair waiting. My family said that they would and not to worry. And I knew that if I had to stop somewhere, I knew where to stop, because I had worked for the Turnpike Authority. I know that every interchange has a handicap bathroom and you can park almost at the door. So I felt that if we had to stop, I could get her into a bathroom or I could get help quickly. All you have to do is hit the code for the Turnpike, and they'll be there really quickly to help you. It was good to know all these safety things were there for us if we needed to use them.

So I felt good coming out the Turnpike with her, and we didn't have any problems. She did really well. She sat there, she talked to me, and we were drinking the water I brought in the car, and we had some grapes and some cheese. And of course we had to have our little candy, because she loves candy. So she had a little bit of that. And she slept quite a bit. But she did very well.

She really enjoyed seeing my son and his wife and of course her great-grandchildren. He has three children, two girls who are five and three and a boy who was not quite a year old when we got out here. He sat on the bed with her and she'd play with him and talk to him, and he was such a good boy. He'd just sat there and listened to her. It was really good and made her so very happy.

I thought if anything could help her and make her smile again, it would be her great-grandchildren.

And the girls were so good to her. They would push her around in the wheelchair, and they'd try to feed her at lunch time. She didn't want to eat much any more and that was one of her biggest problems, getting something in her to eat and drink. I was making all kinds of shakes and putting ice cream in them. I was doing everything I could to try to have her eat more, but she just didn't want to eat. But I would put a supplement powder in the shake and a multivitamin and I would give her some of a healthy antioxidant juice I had in the refrigerator. She was drinking some. So she was getting some good nutrition. And that plus what they gave her there I think is what kept her going from December until July. Her birthday was in March. We had her at my home for her birthday and she looked really pretty in the pictures. We have some good memories from her birthday. She went to blow out the candles to her birthday cake and almost fell face first into her cake. Oh, she laughed and laughed. It was so good to see her laugh. It made my heart so very happy.

She had good days and of course she had bad days. But I was hopeful because she had come back so many times before, like when she was 86 some five years before back in Eastern Pennsylvania.. She had back surgery and afterwards her feet just flopped. She couldn't feel or move them. We didn't think she'd walk again. But within two months, she was walking with these special magnetic technologies from the wellness company I educate people about, Nikken, Inc., as an independent consultant with the company. When I ran our rotating magnetic device for her, she felt tingling and prickling in those dead legs. And we just kept using it. Two months later, she walked out of the nursing home and came home.

And then she had had congestive heart failure and kidney problems. That was from actual surgery and probably too much anesthesia, because she couldn't handle much at her age. And with the heart and the kidneys affected, her heart was now only working at 34 percent, and they told me 50 to 60 percent is pretty normal for someone her age. Six months later, her heart was working at 44 percent. And she was coming back again to walking and getting around. She was amazing.

My mom was 91 when she died. She went into a nursing home after the congestive heart failure and kidney problems. I was actually thinking maybe if I would retire she could come home. But I kept working because I was not old enough at that point to retire.

So when I did retire in December I was 61. When I turned 62, five days later she died. It's good I didn't wait until after my birthday to retire. You never know what would have happened if circumstances had been different. In fact, we much preferred this nursing home in Western Pennsylvania to the one back in Eastern Pennsylvania. Here they were so good to her. For example, they got her out of bed twice a day. They just took such good care of her. And they walked her all the time, anyway they tried to. They were sending her for therapy. Back home in Eastern Pennsylvania they gave up on her. They told me she was dying, and they didn't do much to get her out of bed.

What a difference when we got out here. I know it helped her. And I know her great-grandchildren helped her. And her grandchildren, my son and his wife, were so good to her. They're both in the medical field, so that helped too, because then I did not have to make all the decisions by myself. That's what my son kept saying to me: "Mom, come on out, let us help you." Back home it was just me, because my brother is in Texas and it's just the two of us. So I was trying to work and also be at the nursing home as much as I could be for her, because I knew she was not getting the care that she actually needed. I knew they weren't trying hard enough to feed her. They would come in and they would try. But after a few minutes, they would walk out. Will somebody else come back and try? Well, maybe another nurse will, maybe not. So many times she wouldn't have eaten anything.

I found that if I was there, I was able to get her to eat something. If it was just a milkshake or whatever I made up, or even if it was their shake, I could make sure she drank something. When they came in and they wanted to give her her pills, the nurse would insist that she had to drink her shake to get down the pills. So that was one way we got her to drink a shake. But sometimes for the nurses she would refuse her pills.

Mentally, she was doing well until she was put on a medication in October. It was a beta-blocker, and she can't handle beta-blockers. That seemed to shut down her whole body. After that she just wanted to stay in bed and sleep and didn't want to talk much and didn't want to eat much.

One time they sent her back to the nursing home from the hospital, and they didn't even give her any blood pressure medicine. It wasn't listed. The next day, I was there with her and her blood pressure was going up and up. I said, "What's going on? What is she on?" They went and checked and they had sent her back to the nursing home with no blood pressure medicine.

For twenty years she's been on blood pressure medicine. I said, "Well, we've got to give it to her." They said, "We've got to get something from the doctor first." It's their process, you know. I was ready to go home and get what I had at the house and bring it in. But they finally told me the doctor had ordered it. Then we had to wait for it to be delivered. And now it's the weekend and you know how things move on the weekend - not so good. I was really upset.

And she needed it. I was watching the blood pressure going up and up, and I'm just thinking, oh my gosh. There should be somebody there that can make that decision, that could give her that medicine. But anyway, I learned a lot. I was there a lot. Day and night. I was there a lot at both nursing homes. You learn a lot about what's going on when you're there all the time.

I wasn't a medical person, but I just kept asking questions, and then I'd call my son and his wife and ask them. I had a lot of good friends in my wellness business with Nikken, Inc., whom I could call, and that really helped me too.

I remember at the hospital back East, on one particular Sunday, I was so upset and Mom was doing poorly. I reached in my pocket at the hospital and their in my pocket was a business card of a lady doctor I had met when at a Nikken meeting. I thought, well, why don't I give her a call and see if I could talk to her if she is around? She answered the phone and she talked to me for a good half hour. And she just encouraged me so much to get my mother off of that medicine, that beta-blocker and other medicines they wanted to give her. She said, "She doesn't need that stuff. Not at her age."

Here she was, a doctor of pharmaceuticals, and I thought, isn't it amazing how so many things have happened that show God is in control, like having her card in my pocket that day. And Mom's doctor was giving me such a hard time in the hospital about stopping this medication. He was so mad, he said, "You and your family are absolutely crazy."

But when I talked to this lady doctor who had a degree in pharmaceuticals, she said, "Elaine, you're doing the right thing. Stop the medication. Get her off of it."

So I insisted and the doctor he said, "I'm signing off the case."

I said, "Well that's just fine with me." I figured, there are other doctors. But she made me feel that what we had decided was right. And you know what? Mom did come back after they got her off those medicines and beta-blockers. I got to bring her out here to see her great-grandchildren, in Western Pennsylvania.

She had many good months out here, but she just kept getting more and more tired and didn't want to eat and just wanted to sleep. And I knew she was just wearing out. I think letting go was easier for me in some ways, because I saw the whole process and it took many months. And I was with her when she passed away. So, that made me feel good too, that I could be with her. I held her in my arms as she took her last breath.

I kept telling her, "It's okay, Mom." I love you, Mom. I kept telling her, "It's okay, God's ready for you. It's okay. Go. You be with God." And after she passed I had a really good feeling. I really did. I felt so relieved for her.

My family came in a little bit later, right after that. And I told them, you know, "She's going to be in heaven with my dad and her brothers and her sisters and her mom and her dad." I said, "I think they're going to have one heck of a party up there."

You've just gotta celebrate for them. You've gotta celebrate for them because they're at peace and they're no longer struggling. I don't think she was in pain physically, because she never wanted pain medicine, and she never complained, which was really good. But I think she was just so tired and so worn out.

She was the last of her generation. She was second to the oldest in her family. There were four of them and she was the last one to die.

I just figured I'd try to help her as much as I could. I kept fighting for her, as much as I could to help her, but I knew she wasn't fighting anymore. She didn't even want to drink any more. So I knew that she was giving up basically, and it was hard to see her struggle to drink and breathe. She started having problems in swallowing. Eventually she developed a cough, and I told them I wanted a chest x-ray done. They talked me out of it. They said they didn't think that it was that serious, but it ended up she had pneumonia and that's what took her life. They did the chest x-ray that morning of the 12th. She died that afternoon.

After she died, they told me she had pneumonia. They were giving her breathing treatments after she would eat. Her respiration was very low after she would eat. I would watch her neck and would count her breaths. They would get really fast and then they'd get really slow. She didn't like the breathing treatment. She didn't like that mask on her face. The oxygen she liked better.

I used the Nikken magnetic device on my mom a couple times, because her feet showed signs that things weren't good with circulation. The nurses were telling me, "This isn't good with her feet, and if a clot travels that's not good at all." So I used the device on her legs and it helped with her circulation. It was mostly in her feet where the problem was. But sometimes I'd put the device up near her chest just to try to help her breath a little better, because I have asthma and I know it helps me. I thought, maybe I can help her feel better and breathe better without using all this other stuff that she doesn't like.

She also lay on a magnetic pad from Nikken, Inc., which helped to keep her comfortable and warm enough. She was lying on that and then she had another Nikken comforter on top of her, along with her magnetic pillow. I had a water purity system from Nikken, a little one, in there too. She had her Nikken natural air purifier in there, she had her magnetic necklace on, and she had an energy bracelet most times on one wrist and relaxing magnetic inserts in her shoes when she had them on. So she was drinking good water and was surrounded by energy-building wellness products. When she drank water or I made the shakes, it was always with the purified water from Nikken.

We did try everything possible that we could to help her. Nurses would walk in the room and say, "Boy, there's something about this room. It feels great and smells clean in here." And I know it was the air system. Mom loved her Nikken magnetic products and she took a lot of their nutrition products. She went to a lot of Nikken wellness events with me too. She loved the people in Nikken and they all loved her. They called her Mom. She used the products day and night and she loved to share her experiences with others.

I have no regrets for anything, and I'm so glad I could do everything I did. I think it was a good process for me to go through, and know that she's in a better place.

I know at Christmas when we all got together I was sitting at the table and I thought, "I miss her so much" "Goodness, I'm now the oldest in our immediate family". I really miss my mom. She was also my best friend.

I must admit a lot of my stress has left me, because I was with her all the time. So I worried and didn't sleep the best.

I feel at peace now. I guess that might be the best word to use, because I felt I did everything I could and I have a peace about everything, and it is okay.

It was hard to focus that July after she died. Thank goodness I made some good friends. They'd call me up and say, "Let's go get something to eat." Or, they know I like to dance and we'd go out and go dancing. Or they'd invite me to go to the fair with them or something like that over the summer, which was good, because I can't be relying on my son and his wife and my grandkids all the time. I need another life.

I have my Nikken business, and I've started sharing the technologies with my neighbor and different people. And it's really makes me so happy to see folks getting healthier. I have a lot of new people in my group out here, which is good.

And it's not that I don't miss her. I do miss her everyday. I think of her everyday. But it's just different. You've got to go on, and my family has been so supportive and they take me with them on wonderful vacations. I'm getting time to do different things and I love the Church we all go to together. I have many new adventures and a new outlook on life.

I'm trying other things that I never tried before, because I was working all the time when I worked for the Turnpike. And I had a lot going on with my mom since 2000. She moved in with me in 2000. She was very healthy at that point. She could out-walk me because of my asthma. She was what I would call a "schussel," if you know what that is in German or Pennsylvania Dutch. It's someone who scurries around really fast and can knock things over because she moves too fast. My dad always called her a schussel. She was a fast-moving person and always cleaning. She always had a broom or a mop or a dust rag or something in her hand, and she loved to cook. So she was always very, very active, and always helped others.

My father died in December of 1996, a few days before Christmas. He was in a nursing home, but he was doing fairly well until he got a bad cold and the flu, and three days later he died.

So that hit really fast. And my mom had a public sale July of the next year and she moved into a senior high-rise building. I knew she wasn't happy there. When I had my fusion surgery to my neck in 2000, it was winter time. After I came home from the hospital, I needed to stay home and rest. I said to her, "Why don't you come over and stay with me? It's no use for you to be stranded at your house and me be stranded here. You're worrying about me and I'm worrying about you. Why don't you just come and stay with me?"

So she came over and stayed with me until I got better. And we got along really well, so we decided to look for a home together. I was looking at half of a duplex, but what we ended up with was a rancher. Her bedroom was at one end, and then the living room, dining room, and kitchen were in the middle, and then on the other end were two bedrooms and a bath, where I was. One bedroom was my office and the other was my bedroom. It worked out really well, because we had enough personal space for each of us.

I worked night shift on the Turnpike, which was 11:00 pm at night till 7:00 am in the morning. And I'd come in each morning and she'd be getting up at 7:30 or 8:00 am. She'd be getting her bath and getting dressed when I came in, and I'd go lay down about 8:00, and sometimes I was up by 12:00 or 1:00. I tried to sleep till 3:00. Once I got the Nikken magnetic sleep system for myself, then I could really sleep, especially with the Nikken sleep mask over my eyes. That mask really helped me a lot to keep the room dark and just to relax me more.

The sleep system helped with my asthma and sinuses too. I was on eight medications when I started my wellness program and three months later I was only taking one medication. Today I have my inhaler in my purse and that's it. Now I am being more careful with my eating, avoiding sugar, and eating lots of vegetables.

As for my feelings now after some time has passed, I miss her very much everyday and a day does not go by that I don't think about her. She was my best friend as well as my mom. They say time erases everything. Not everything, but a lot of the pain. You get better. I just remember the memories. All the good times we had together.

I like to think of her 91st birthday party. She was dressed so pretty and she looked so beautiful, not 91 years old. We had the cake and we had the candles, but not 91 of them! I remember she went to blow out the candles and she bent over to blow them out and she almost fell forward. She was going to fall into the cake, but I caught her just in time. And she laughed and she laughed and she laughed. I will forever remember that moment and the smile on her face. I got a great picture of her with my daughter-in-law.

I kind of wish I would have been in that position and some one else would have been taking the picture, so that the picture would be of my mom and me. But that's okay. I have lots of pictures of us both. And it all happened the way it was supposed to be, because I was the one that got to her to catch her before she fell in the cake. I saw her coming forward and I grabbed her or she would have fallen right into the candles and into the cake. I was so grateful just to see her laugh and enjoy that moment.

It was just uncontrollable laughter and she was just so happy and just having so much fun. Later we tried to take some pictures with all of us and she was too tired.

Another memory is with the girls, my two grand-daughters. We'd go into the nursing home and we'd sing "Old MacDonald Had a Farm" to her. Sometimes it was in the dining room because we couldn't get her awake when we wanted to feed her. So we'd be singing this song and then we'd get to the chicken in the song, and I'd say, "Mom, chicken. How does a chicken go?" And she'd go, "Bawk, bawk-bawk, bawk-bawk." And we would laugh and laugh. I'd laugh and all the people in the dining room would laugh. After a while, other people were helping us sing.

It was just a great moment for everybody. And even at times when we were in her room and the kids were there – maybe she just wanted to keep her eyes closed – I'd start singing that song and the kids would too. And now they talk about it. They talk about Gigi – that's what they called her – and they talk about the song and Old MacDonald and how she made the noises. And you know what? She got the noises right too. At 91 she got every sound right. So you know the mind was still working!

As people age they just go back to being a kid. They raise us and then we have to take over and we have to help them as they go back and they decline and more or less become like a child again.

I just did fun things with my mom and incorporated my family as much as I could, especially the children. Because I know the great-grandchildren will always remember those moments. I know they will because they keep talking about it.

At the cemetery they let balloons go, three of them, one for each of the three great-grandchildren, and they wrote a note to her. And we were all standing there watching the balloons go up higher and higher and higher, until we couldn't see them anymore.

People took pictures of us and those pictures are nice to look at, because it brings back what we were doing and why we were looking up. And the balloons are going to heaven and isn't that where she was? For the children, we could explain it to them better. The balloons were going to her.

It was good. I think we did some wonderful things. Their mother thought of the balloons and I thought that was a good idea for the kids.

I remember things my mom did that I can appreciate more now. My mom just loved to cook and clean and do all that kind of stuff. She wasn't much of a gardener, but she liked her plants in her house. Her whole thing was the cooking and the cleaning and just taking care of the laundry in the house. I appreciated her cooking – I miss some of the good food personally. She was a very good cook.

Sometimes when I cook one of Mom's favorite meals, my son and his wife say, "That smells just like Grandma and her cooking." Or I'll take something over to their house and they'll say, "Oh, that's good. I remember when Grandma made that."

She came back from so many bad situations. My son is a physician's assistant and it impressed my son so much when she could walk again. And his wife is a physical therapist assistant. When they saw her in the hospital after that back surgery with the drop foot and her feet just flopping, they said to me, "I don't think she will ever walk again." And two months later she was walking.

They couldn't believe it. My son is in dermatology, so like he says, he was not that familiar with the details of my mom's medical issues. But he would get on the computer and he'd read and let me know different things. Or if I told him about a medication, he'd get online and look it up, and then he'd tell me what he thought of it and if she needed it or who I needed to talk to about it. So he helped me in a lot of ways over the years with a lot of different things. And for them, they have those memories of her coming back. He often says, "I just can't believe how Grandma came back so many times from different serious situations, how she walked again and recovered after the congestive heart failure and kidney problems." Even her kidney doctor was impressed. .

There are different things I remember. I appreciate so much everything that she did, because now I'm in charge basically to keep memories going, to keep some of those good dinners going. And even with the little ones, there were certain things she made for them that they really enjoyed, and I want to keep that going. My son is a great cook too. He cooks all organic and has a home focused on wellness and they all sleep on the magnetic sleep systems. I'm so proud of where they've gone from where they were.

My granddaughter, the oldest one, who is six years old now, had open heart surgery before she was two. And her parents know that their efforts to keep her healthy as an infant helped tremendously.

Children are wonderful, the way they're resilient and how they come back from these situations. Talk about memories and something that stays in your mind! That sure stays in your mind. After her surgery how she wanted to play with our name tags and how she laughed and smiled. She just bounced back so quickly, it was just amazing.

Like my mom, her great-grandma. She's small, and petite, but she just goes and goes and goes, with energy plus. She loves sports and is very competitive. Her sister is more like me; she loves to eat, sometimes too much. They're good kids. And then their little brother, oh, my goodness! He is such a joy!

At the viewing he ran to me across the room and I picked him up and he gave me a big hug. It just melts your heart, you know. The kids, how good they were through that whole process with my mom. And with the other ladies and men at the nursing home, how the girls would go around and talk to them and visit with them.

When I think about my mom and my own experience and now my son's family, I really appreciate the mothers in the world, and the dads. And when I look at these little children and how we influence them and what their parents are doing to give them a good life and take them to church and teach them what's right and wrong; that was my mom. She was with my son a lot because I worked. His dad wasn't involved in his life much at all after he was five. So my parents did a lot for him. They were very close.

So to see him now with his children, I see a lot in him that maybe my mom would have done. And then I see my daughter-in-law and the good mom she is and how good they are with the children. Family just means so much. At one point I think in our lives, or in my life anyway, maybe I didn't get it as good as I get it now. But family is what it's all about. It really is.

So I listen to my family and I spend time with them. That's what I'm trying to do for my grandchildren - just be there. I play with them, I'll play tag, and we'll play magic wand, and they make me a witch and then I have to go after them as a witch, and that's okay. They find all these wonderful things that I need to be and I need to chase them around in the basement.

I just take the time and spend time, and my mom did that. My mom did that with my son and she did that with me when I was growing up. She took time. And I remember many times she was out playing ball with me. I loved to play ball and sports. I was always into one sport or another. I remember the fun things she'd like to do, like go to carnivals and go to the swimming pool. She liked to have fun. And she liked to take me special places. She was so good to me.

My dad was more stern and serious. He worked so much I don't remember him being home that much. But my mom was home more and loved to have fun. So she was definitely the person to take me places and do things. And I see the things my son and his wife do with their kids. It's not all about how much money you spend on them; it's what you do with them and the quality of time that you spend with them.

I gave the girls each a coloring book for Valentine's Day, and they just thanked me and thanked me and thanked me for a dollar coloring book. They both love to color and I thought, boy, I couldn't have bought a better gift. We sat down and we colored together. So it's taking the time to do that, and I saw that in my mom and I see that in my son and his wife. You've got to take time for your family and your friends and the people that mean the most to you.

I'm very impressed with the dad my son has become, because he didn't have a lot of that role model in his life. He had a grandpa but he didn't have a dad around too much. I'm proud of him for the dad he has become. He loved his grandma and she loved him. They did so much together and she played with him all the time and spoiled him but that is what grandparents are for.

We all carry certain things that we need to get rid of and just deal with and then you can move forward so much better. You can become a better person. And I think that attending personal growth programs has just opened me up.

At one time I wouldn't talk much about my feelings or anything like that. I listened but I wouldn't say much about things. I think these programs really helped me to open up and just grow as a person.

We're all together. This is what's happening around us. We're basically all in the same situation. We have feelings and we want love and we want support and caring and compassion in our life. I really want to make a difference in people's lives. I love sharing the Nikken wellness technologies. When people get better I feel such a joy in my heart for them. I love what I do.

My mom was a stay at home mom when I was little, up until I went to school, and then she worked down the street in the shoe factory. It was a couple of blocks from where I was in school. My grandma lived a half a block from the school. So after school I would go to my grandma's and my mom would come and get me after work. My mom's education was through eighth grade. I was very proud of her. I had a farmer's market business with a bakery and a deli in Eastern Pennsylvania, and she came to help me out. And she was adding on the paper whatever they'd buy. We had a cash drawer, not a cash register, so we had to give change and she got very good at doing that. She was quite the sales lady. She would say, "Oh, this is so delicious. This is just so good – I love it." What are you gonna do? You're gonna buy, right?

She loved the pastries. I was really proud of her for what she accomplished later in life. In the beginning she was very nervous but she got very good at it.

She was such a hard worker in so many ways at the shoe factory and at the house. There are many times I'll just sit and close my eyes and go back to that house that I grew up in and just try to remember room by room what it was like, because they are such good memories.

My dad had a few more years of schooling, but I know he didn't graduate either. But he was lucky – he got into business for himself, and he did really well with that. He had a gas station and a trailer park. That's where I think I learned my skills. I can pretty much talk to anyone because of my dad, the sales person. My dad had a delivery route selling frozen foods when I was first married. I would go with him on his route and help him.

We could knock on twice as many doors that way. My dad taught me so much. I mean, we had a cherry tree in our backyard with big bing cherries, and he had me out door to door going down the street, selling those from a wagon when I was six or seven years old.

Back then kids could do that, and you didn't have to worry about them knocking on the doors. My dad was the entrepreneur, where my mom was the homemaker and kept things going at the house. I thought it was a great balance as I got older.

I remember my dad had a motorcycle with a side car. So Mom and I would sit in the side car when I was young and we would go for a Sunday drive. I can still remember waving to the people as we drove by. And how dad would take us for a watermelon and that was such a treat. They had big tubs of ice water with the watermelons floating around in it. They would plug a watermelon and show you the heart so you could see if it was good and ripe.

I don't remember my mom sitting down much at all. I remember she was really sick one time. I was really young and when I saw her in the hospital I thought she was going to die. She went to the hospital for surgery for a hysterectomy and gallbladder. I was so sad and crying and didn't want to go home with my dad. I wanted to stay with my mom and take care of her.

I remember the little day bed in the dining room, with her lying there and then getting sick with the gallstones, and after supper she had to go upstairs and get sick. And she'd ask me to go downstairs and get her something to drink and it was her "medicine." It was actually Porter beer. My mom liked a beer every day. She would drink Porter beer, and the doctor would say, "If you can keep it down, there's good stuff in there. You drink your beer." She loved her beer. She was a character.

I think I went through all the stages of grief. I did a lot of that before she died, when she was so sick. I wanted her to come back and I wanted her to get stronger. I can remember when I was taking her for a drive and was talking to her, and I pleaded with her and begged her. "Mom, come on. You've got to eat, you've got to drink. You won't live if you don't eat and drink." And she wouldn't talk. She wouldn't say much at all to me. She'd just sit there and look at me and I was just pleading with her to please, please eat and drink.

So I think there were stages I went through before her passing. And then I think I finally accepted the fact that she just couldn't eat and drink anymore and that this was my way of knowing her life was coming to an end. I remember at the funeral I kept telling myself that this is about her today. Think about her life. Be happy for her and her life. Don't have tears. Be happy. But it was hard.

It was really hard. And it still gets hard.

I have to tell you my mom was a Moravian and the Moravian Church has a Moravian star. They're really popular. A lot of people put them up at Christmas time outside. Well, last year when we moved here, I noticed just one Moravian star around the town. But recently, I'm coming out of my development here where I live, and in front of me is a landscaping business. They had all these Moravian stars. If there was one, there were twenty of them hanging there all lit up, all aglow. It was like, "Oh, my goodness." Tears ran down my cheeks, because it was like my mom was right there.

I fixed the one bedroom up here when I moved in here, really for her, and I brought a lot of her things when I moved. I had to make a lot of decisions even then, because we had moved out here permanently. I could only bring so much.

I still have some boxes out in the garage that are Mom's and that I need to go through. And I have a big hutch in the living room that has her shoe collection in it. She collected the little porcelain shoes from everywhere we went and some antique ones, and people would give them to her because they all knew she collected them. And we have a lot of beer mugs, because I was in Germany the first year I was married and she came over to visit us.

I remember my daughter-in-law saying to me when we were unpacking, "Are we going to keep all this stuff?"

I said, "Yeah. Those boxes are each marked with what shelf their contents go on. There are five or six shelves where the shoes go. Shelf one, two, three – start at the top. Just put it on that shelf."

It's hard. It's so hard. I was so glad my aunt was there with me as I was going through her jewelry. My aunt and I went through most of her jewelry back home before we came here, and most of it I brought with me. It was nice for my aunt to sit down and do that with me. I thanked her. I said, "I'm so glad I have somebody here with me. And it's you. You don't know what this means to me." As we were going through these things, she would remember some of the things that Mom would wear. And she'd say, "Oh, I remember seeing her in this." So it was good. It felt really good.

My only brother is in Texas with his wife, and they weren't here when I moved all this stuff out here to Western Pennsylvania. My brother has been so very sick. He did come back home for the funeral. He ended up in the hospital when he got back to Texas. He has a bad infection in his lungs and many complications, even requiring brain surgery. At Christmas I didn't even know if I'd be here or in Texas because he was very, very sick. I feel so bad for his wife because I know how hard it is. I know she's in the hospital with him and moving from one hospital to the next. He's seven years older than I am. I try to keep in contact and help however I can over the phone. I pray for his healing.

The most surprising feeling I experienced with my mom was the anger. She wouldn't eat. I didn't want her to see how upset and angry I was. But I wanted her to know how important it was for her to eat and drink.

I said, "Mom, I wouldn't be telling you this and I wouldn't be talking to you about it if I didn't care. I wouldn't say anything to you. I'd just let you go and let you not eat and drink." I said, "It's so hard for me to sit here and you don't eat and drink anything." I didn't say it in front of everybody, just to her.

Sometimes she'd say, "I'll do better," or something. And then there were times she didn't talk, sometimes for days, about anything, She wouldn't talk.

So there are times when I got angry. I would go out to the car sometimes and just sit out there, and I would pound on the steering wheel because I was angry. I just cried and cried. But I waited till I got out there to just get rid of my anger and frustrations.

My advice to other mothers losing their mothers is to just spend as much time with them as you can, and try to share memories. I had a lot of pictures, and Mom and I looked at a lot of pictures together. And that way I got her to talk and asked her who they were in the pictures or where it was.

We watched Dean Martin's DVDs, and we'd laugh and laugh. She liked how he always jumped on top of the piano. She loved music and always had it playing in her room.

Michael Jackson's funeral was the day of my birthday and I was sitting there in the nursing home watching the funeral, thinking this is too sad, I don't want to watch this. My mom was pretty bad that day too. And I thought, oh, this is too much for me for this one day.

I pushed her around in the wheelchair outside and took her for walks too, and so did the kids. We would go outside as much as we could. She loved the flowers that they had planted at the facility, so we'd go looking for flowers. And I'd take her for drives in the car. They would help me load her in the car and help me get her out. I'd take her for drives and take her to look at the beautiful flowers when all the hydrangeas and different flowers were blooming.

I just think you should get as many good memories as you can and help them to have some good laughs and be happy. Let them know how special they are to you. I always told her how much I loved her, many times a day.

There's no going back – death is so final.

This interview has been good. And in parts of it, of course, I've had tears, but it's good to talk. I appreciate this a lot because it is so good to share our stories, and it helped to take me through some of this process, which is good.

I think we need to hear from other people about what they're going through, because everything we share helps somebody. And I think that's what this book will do. I think it will help lots of ladies who have lost their moms.

I hope we can help a lot of people, and it will be interesting to read some of the other ladies' thoughts and what they have to share too. I think it's going to be good for everybody.

It's cleansing. It's peaceful. We have to share, we have to talk, we have to let go.

And you just feel more at peace after it's over.

Whenever I talk about my mom, for the longest time my oldest granddaughter, the six year old, would look at me to see if I had tears. She looks at me this certain way. She has this smile on her face, but it's just such a different look in her face, the grin on her face. And I'll say, "Oh, I'm fine, I'm fine." Both girls have been very supportive, with me talking and playing with them. That helps. That helps tremendously, just being able to be with my grandkids and my son and his wife.

I'm so glad that I had at least one child. I wanted more, but it never happened. So I just have to be thankful for what I have. And I am. I feel I'm very blessed. I have been very blessed all my life. We all have trials and tribulations and we all have tough times in our lives. I think we grow through all that. We grow tremendously through all that.

Thank you. I hope I help people somehow. If just one word helps someone else, that's good.

Making the decision to have a child – it's momentous. It is to decide forever to have your heart go walking around outside your body.
ELIZABETH STONE

CHAPTER 7

THE IMPORTANCE OF YOUR FEELINGS

The stories you are hearing in this book are the stories of women like you, who are not afraid to face their feelings, who are deeply thoughtful and understanding about their relationships with their mothers, who are sensitive to the differences between their lifestyles and their mothers' lifestyles, and who are loving, forgiving, and grateful. They are simply grieving, mourning, and processing the meaning of their mother's life, its meaning for them, and the insights which that process adds to their experience of life now, as a mother, as woman, and as a human being.

I believe that as a culture, we focus much too much on family pathology and not enough on what a healthy, meaningful, thoughtful relationship looks like. My parenting books, for instance, have always aimed to show how to build a healthy family relationship rather than focusing on fixing damaged ones. Hopefully by reading the stories here in *Mothers Losing Mothers* you will be reinforced in your own healthy process, as well as be touched, moved, inspired, amused, and comforted along the way.

I am overwhelmed by my admiration for these wonderful women who opened their hearts to me and so frankly shared their most intimate moments, memories, and feelings with me in hopes of giving other mothers some comfort and guidance through a very difficult time in your life. I hope you will benefit as I did from their most generous and fruitful sharings.

Your feelings are your own and are to be trusted

What are the words we use to describe what we feel? I overflowed with inconsolable tears when I finally named my feeling – it was like wandering in an empty castle. I still well up when I speak or write the words. There are so many words we use, but few can suffice. It may help you to find your own image for what it is you are feeling. Is it a bridge, an ocean, a beached whale, a side-tracked train, an empty plate, a winter tree bereft of leaves, a rudderless ship, a space probe cut off from earth, a quiet meadow, a forest glen, or a moonlit night?

Or is it grief, lament, mourning, loss, pain, tragedy, emptiness, loneliness, aloneness, bereavement, despair, being orphaned, left behind, abandoned, free fall, anguish, depression, pity, woe, sorrow, heartache, misery, angst, trial, torture, distress, torment, anxiety, suffering, agony, affliction, ordeal, trouble, tribulation, testing, nightmare, trauma, hurting, sting, transition, transformation, enlightenment? I have heard all these and more from mothers losing mothers.

But none and all describe what we feel at one time or another in the first days, weeks, months, and years. We also feel numb, paralysis, ossification, anger, and lots more. Our language gives us ways to identify our feelings so that we can look at them, accept them for what they are, and let them pass. New feelings will replace them, absolutely, if we simply own them and let them pass.

If this kind of loss is inevitable, that is, even if everything goes right in your life you still must endure the loss of your mother and the unknown losses or missed opportunities for your children or grandchildren, we may be forced to ask, is life just "a veil of tears" after all?

I think this question is central to our process of dealing with our mother's death. What is it all for? It is said that a special characteristic of the human spirit is the need to find purpose. We look for causes and effects. We want to believe we can make things happen, we can learn things, we can alter our environment and our circumstances for the good of ourselves and those we love. We want to find meaning beyond our immediate circumstances. We feel religious feelings because we want to believe it is all for a higher purpose that we live. For those who reject a religious solution, we still seek purpose in evolution, progress, science, understanding, exploration, compassion, the human experience.

Why is this natural process so painful?

So why if this is the way it is supposed to be is there so much pain? I offer this solution: It is precisely because it makes us ask this question. The pain is so deep because it makes us ask not just why we are here but why our mother was here, what was the meaning, or meanings, of her life? And how are we meant to make it all meaningful into the future?

If the pain is inevitable, perhaps it is up to us to create the joy, the blessings, the happiness, the fun, the love, the enthusiasm, the glory, the goodness, which makes life worthwhile! How do we carry forward what our mother gave us – the gift of life?

Perhaps it is up to us to find the solace to overcome the sadness – to find the sympathy, the consolation, the comfort, the pleasure, the renewal, the healing which we need and which we can pass on to others. I believe that in profound sadness, there is a feeling of surrender and awe which can give us more power, and better direction, and a sense of serenity and fulfillment.

In a rare article about the loss of close family members which appeared in the *New York Times*, February 26, 2011,[8] authors Meghan O'Rourke and Joyce Carol Oates shared their thoughts, the former having lost her mother when she was 30 and the later having lost her husband. O'Rourke called this feeling of surrender a "note of recognition and relinquishment."

Motherhood may be the ultimate expression of the continuity of spirit through the lives of generation after generation. Just as our lives keep changing through various stages, so do our feelings. I propose that it is precisely because we are mature women with the

---

[8] Joyce Carol Oates and Meghan O'Rourke, "Why We Write About Grief," *The New York Times*, 26 February 2011, Week in Review, http://www.nytimes.com/2011/02/27/weekinreview/27grief.html?pagewanted=all.

experience of being mothers that the loss of our mother is so deeply moving for us. We bring so much to it. We have lived in the castle, we have built our own castle, and now we see that castles, no matter how well fortified or how elegant, do not last forever. Ours too will crumble. So it is only what we create through spirit which will last. It is what we give our children which will give meaning to our lives and to the lives of our mothers.

The effects can be truly global in our lives

For each of us our reaction to the loss of our mother is uniquely our own. Of course there is much we all have in common as women and mothers of our generation, but because we and our mothers are each a unique expression of the human experience, our reactions can vary widely. Of course there is sadness, grief, and mourning, but there can also be confusion, regrets, floods of unique memories, moments of clarity and moments of utter obscurity, times of numbness and times of hyperactivity, vacillations between despair and hope, glimpses of understanding followed by mysterious gulfs of ignorance.

Yet it seems clear that the effects are global. Every area of our lives is changed, sometimes a little, sometimes a lot, but nevertheless changed. Little things can become more important while things which seemed critical get pushed aside.

For example, our financial circumstances can change, either up or down. This can be a direct result of our mother's death, because of money we spent on our mother's behalf or money we received on her passing. Or it can be indirect, because of our own shifting priorities. Perhaps we decide to change careers or downsize our home or go back to school. Perhaps we decide to become more responsible savers or investors. Perhaps we decide to shift priorities for our children and pay more towards schooling or less on other activities, or vice versa. Maybe we quit a job to have more time with our families or we go after a long delayed dream of work, travel, or service.

Many families have extra costs because of caring for an aging parent, while others find their lives change dramatically when they gain an inheritance. Sometimes our finances can go from one extreme to the other as a result of both circumstances. This was true for me. I am self-employed as a writer and educator and I had much less time to build my business in the last two years of my mother's life because she needed me more and more. But then when she passed on, I suddenly had a significant fund which I had to figure out how to manage and allocate. My feelings about this shift can be at times almost as confusing and disturbing as the feelings generated directly by the pain and sadness of the loss of my mother.

Major shifts at all levels

Like financial shifts, relationship shifts can be huge when our mother dies. How do we see our children now, now that we are no longer someone's child? What role does our husband or partner now play in our lives, now that our elders are departing? Will we rely on his insights more, or less?

In most cases I find that all personal relationships seem to become more important than they were before, though if you had asked before, that would have seemed impossible. I have always maintained that my family relationships were top priority. But now, every second seems even more precious and the profound value of time with family is dramatically affirmed.

How much effort we put into our careers changes too. If we feel our work is valuable and adds to our community we may dedicate more of ourselves to it. If we are not fulfilled by our work or don't feel that we are contributing value, we may pull back and work less hard at perfecting our performance. We may feel closer to nature, take vacations more seriously, or take up some hobby which never appealed to us before but was a favorite of our mother's, and suddenly we get the urge to try it.

Change is inevitable, so you may as well embrace it and explore it with an open mind to grasp its lessons for your growth and future happiness, as have the wonderful ladies whose stories you are benefiting from as you turn these pages.

There's a lot more to being a woman than being a mother, but there's a hell of a lot more to being a mother than most people suspect.
ROSEANNE BARR

CHAPTER 8

MARY ANN'S STORY: EMERALD JUNGLE

I'm ready to talk about my mom. I have a glass of water and I'm going to sit down and look out my windows. My mother actually died the day of her 89th birthday, which was May 13th, 2009.

It was really interesting. When you look at the cards that we had for the service, you see "May 13th, 1920 to May 13th, 2009." It really hit me when I looked at it. How many people have that kind of symmetry in their life?

My father is 91 and he had his 91st birthday on May 5th. So he had his 90th birthday, unfortunately, when my mom was still alive but going through the throes of her last weeks on this earth. So we tried to do something to celebrate it, and we did. We had a little reception for him. But obviously it was hard to be celebrating his success reaching that mark when his wife was in final respite care.

He's doing really, really well. I think my father is a pretty resilient, tough guy. I think all of us had thought that my mom would be the one that would outlive him, but I guess we forgot to look at constitution. My father is pretty stubborn and pretty resilient, and my mother actually comes totally from love.

It's an interesting thing, what keeps us going on this earth. It's one of those things that you take a look at. Now it's hitting me how we are the holder of the legacy at this point with our moms being gone. It's interesting that I'm also having my first grandchild. September 20th is the due date, and I'm going to be in my mother's role for the first time, a year after she left. I have a feeling that she gifted this whole process by sending that child.

I have one child, JT, and he purchased a hotel in Costa Rica when he was 31. So he's living there. That's who I'm going to see when I leave on Tuesday, so I can see his wife pregnant before the baby is born, and I'm sure we'll also visit them again after the birth.

An interesting thing about this is that the last picture we have of my mom was the day before she had her aneurysm, and she was at that time in Costa Rica with me and my father and my son. The last picture we have of her is one my son took with his phone, and she's hugging Katerine, his wife, who is the one who's ready to have our first grandchild. It's such an adorable picture, because they both come from the same kind of energy. They both come from this very loving, uncomplicated energy. And you can almost see it in the picture, and that's the last photo we have.

You can feel the energy between the two of them. And it was very important to my mom that she go see her grandson JT on that visit. My brother Raymond and I have shared about this since. He's working with me in my wellness business. He feels that my mother had some kind of awareness that things weren't 100 percent right, whether it was just feeling maybe a little out of bounds sometimes walking or maybe feeling a little more of a tendency towards high blood pressure, even though she really had very little of that.

I think being an aware person who was just really in tune with her body, she just didn't want to lay her concerns on us. Looking back on it, we both feel that she also had an awareness that there were certain things she wanted to have happen before it was all over. And one of them was visiting my son and meeting Katerine. Katerine couldn't come here because she doesn't have a visa as yet to travel to the United States. She had a passport and can go everywhere other than the United States. Isn't that interesting?

The reason they make it so hard for people from Central America and Mexico to come here is because of the whole illegal immigrants issue. They have to show that they have so much income and property and so on. And Katerine and JT aren't married as yet because he's just two years out of a divorce and so it's one of those things where he's feeling that once the child is born the child can go to the U.S. because the child will have dual citizenship and then they can get the baby's passport and get her visa at the same time. But it's one of those things: My mom went there to see them, and that's where she had her aneurysm. I think she went there specifically to see Katerine, because she had an awareness that she might never get to see her otherwise.

That's Monday morning quarterbacking and there are some things we might have said or done if we had let our own awareness really become more conscious, but I don't think those are the kinds of things our moms want us to hold on to, simply because we had a little bit of denial.

Out of love they basically want to pass without burdening anyone – the thing about women on the whole is that we are kind of geared up to really not impact many people with our own needs. So this has actually taught me something. In fact, I was just recently at a business expo where I had the only wellness booth. There was a woman three booths down who had done something to her eye and it was really obvious. She was selling sheets there, and she felt she needed to stay there. I said to her, "You know, your eye is really, really important. And I would hate to think that you stayed all day doing this and then had to drive home three hours, when you should be taking care of your eye. Don't do what a lot of women do." She said that there was another booth from her company where they had two people, but they both were needed at that booth.

I said, "So you don't have any value?" It was like she was so concerned about how they were doing that she wasn't going to take care of her eye. Well, after talking to me she actually called them. She was from out of town so I said, "There's a booth from American Red Cross in the next aisle. Why don't you go ask them for local connections?"

She ended up seeing an eye doctor. She had scratched her cornea, and the doctor said, "It was so good you came now, because if you hadn't, you could have done damage to your eye."

Afterwards, she said to me, "Thank you for being so concerned about me."

And I said, "Yeah, of course. We women are horrible. We come last all the time." I think that one of the things my mother is sending me messages about, is to be more in balance that way, to understand that there are times when it is good to be thinking of the needs of others, but not at the expense of something that is really near and dear to us, like our eyesight.

After my mom's passing, my responsibilities really started impacting me in many, many ways. She was traveling with me to Costa Rica. My husband was home and we were in Costa Rica staying in the jungle basically. We weren't too far away from civilization, but the night this happened we had just had a great dinner – my father, she and I, and Katerine and JT. She had had her first Mojito and loved it! We were at JT and Katerine's hotel, which is in the rain forest, and there was a torrential rainstorm. The hotel has an open-air lobby, so the rain caused some flooding that was affecting their lobby. My son has two dogs that stay at the hotel, so I said, "Mom, let's take the dogs and get them out of the confusion." We figured we'd drive back to the house where we were staying in the jungle and get out of their way and let the storm continue.

When we got out of the car at the house, there was a lot of flooding near the river near where the house was. So we had to walk through up to mid-shin water to get to the house, and my mother had concerns about her balance. It was pretty dramatic. There was not a lot of great lighting in the jungle in a storm. I don't know if that experience had to do somewhat with the pressure she was feeling that caused the aneurysm in her brain, but when we got to the house, we were hanging up our raincoats. My mother brought one out to my father who was out on the deck, for him to hang it up, and she fell. We thought it was because she had slipped, but it turns out that she probably had the aneurysm just then and that's why she fell.

So basically from there, there were decisions that had to be made. Being in a country that I wasn't that familiar with and having no phone coverage there, I got in the car to drive back to the hotel to get JT involved. Because of the storm and probably because of my panic, two of the car wheels on one side went off the edge of a bridge I was crossing, and the car was tipped over the river. So I had to try to climb out of the car.

You would never know how much strength it takes to climb out of a car that's tipped the other way, even just to try to open the door that is hung so that it closes. And I've been a muscle builder. But you're pushing a heavy door up, against gravity. It took all my strength just even to get out of the car. Of course I knew which direction I had to go, because if I climbed out the other way, the car might have flipped into the water!

I was making all the right decisions that I was aware I had to make for myself, but once I got out of the car, I went through waist deep water in a skirt, with sandals which I obviously took off. So there I am walking barefoot on roads and all these other things, in the dark, in torrential rain, to go back to the house, to get the neighbor who I knew was very well connected, to see what he could do about getting an ambulance and to call JT. There was no way I was going to make it back to the hotel without the car.

It was now late at night, the neighbors were in bed, I woke them up, and they did help me. Why I didn't go there to begin with is again that female thing, I think, that you're not supposed to inconvenience others, you know. I was going to take care of it myself instead of waking them up, right? It's a theme, isn't it?

When I was forced to do it I did it, because it was all about my mom. When we did get the neighbors and the ambulance there, obviously they were concerned. They didn't realize it was a stroke or an aneurysm. They were really thinking that she might have broken something in her neck or in her spine. So they braced her for that, and she had to go over these bumpy roads, and they had to get past my car which was half stuck on the bridge. It was really dramatic.

My son was there in the ambulance, and we had to go to this clinic that was nearby. This is a resort town, so they had only a clinic. There they said, "She needs to have x-rays because of her age, in case she broke anything." So we had to go in an ambulance to Limon, and my son said, "I need to get your car out. I need to take care of a bunch of things. So Mom, you're just going to have to go from here without me." I don't speak Spanish, but I thought, "Okay, it's what has to happen, I'll do it, I'll manage it somehow."

So we went to the hospital in Limon, and when I was in the emergency room I understood why my son didn't want to go with us, because they usually kick everyone out anyhow. They didn't want me to stay with her.

I said, "There's no way I'm leaving my mother!" I said, "She's almost 89 years old. She's visiting this country. She doesn't speak Spanish. She's never been ill, and I'm not leaving her." So they sent a security guard after me, and I said the same thing to the security guard. They probably didn't understand a single word of English, but certainly they understood my face and expression and demeanor. He walked away and left me there.

They wanted me to wait outside. I'm still in wet clothing, now exposed to air-conditioning, and my mother is freezing too. So I'm trying to find extra blankets to put on her. And at this point she's still talking to me, but there are things that are going on, like obviously her brain was filling with blood. But they said, "We're sending you in an ambulance now to go to San Jose. There are no broken bones."

I said to my mom, "Well Mom, the good thing is you didn't break your hip or anything, so there's not going to be any complications there. You've had a stroke and it's going to take some rehab. At least you're not going to deal with any broken bones." And she said, "Of course not. I'm taking your OsteoDenx bone complex." That's the nutritional supplement for bone health we distribute in my independent wellness business with Nikken, Inc. She's still the little Nikken Silver distributor.

So anyway, we make it to the hospital in San Jose; she's still conscious. Now this all started at 10 o'clock at night, and now it's around 11 o'clock in the morning. And I haven't been in bed, and I haven't eaten. I got one bottle of water that I had to go outside to get from a vendor before the ambulance left, and I was trying to feed my mom some water.

When we get to the hospital they do the CAT scan, and my mom and I are talking, and they're asking her if she knows my name. She says, "Of course, it's Mary Ann." And she's counting. She's counting, "One, two ..." and she goes all the way to 350. She was trying to stay with it. She felt she was losing her brain, so she was trying to stay here, present. She wanted to prove to herself she was still okay, she was trying to keep herself focusing on something.

It was pretty amazing to be there with her. They eventually got her into ICU, and they showed me the x-rays. I was with her in ICU and it was getting to be about 7 o'clock at night. I did find a doctor there who actually took me to find a restaurant. She was amazing. She was kind of an angel. I actually called her to let her know I'm coming into Costa Rica next week. Every time I needed something in that hospital I would find her. She was everywhere I needed someone. Every time, no matter where I was in the hospital, there she was. And she spoke English.

Then my mom actually had a major stroke. Unfortunately, I left to go get some sleep, while the rest of the family was coming in two hours later. We got a hotel that I went to and I fell asleep, because I hadn't had any sleep in more than 24 hours. So basically, my mother had the stroke that really took her down when I was in bed that night. When we went down the next morning they told us that she had had a major stroke, which is apparently pretty common, because from what I understand, if you have vascular issues and some of your capillaries are destroyed with a cerebral hemorrhage like she had, this puts too much pressure on the other tissues and oftentimes there is a second stroke which is huge. I think those are very hard to stop, because they're not like the strokes that come from a blockage. In fact, in this situation, they can't give you the medication that dilutes things so that you don't have another one, because it would actually make you bleed more.

So by the time JT and my dad and everyone were there with me, she was pretty much unconscious in a coma. She did come out of the coma over time. The care at that hospital in Costa Rica was amazing: they celebrate the small things that happen when people recover there. What I got to see is the difference between our healthcare systems in Costa Rica, from a social and spiritual and personal perspective: between the way they deal with recovery there and the way we do here in the United States. I got to witness it, because I remember vividly being in the ward. They were taking such good care of her and they would say, "You should have seen your mom today. She looked right at us." They were just talking about every little change in her. They would say, "Look at your mom. On the whole ward of people that have strokes, she is the only one that's now breathing on her own. Look at how she's making all of this recovery." My mother would be hearing this, of course, because apparently the last thing that goes is hearing. She was seeing their smiling faces and all the happiness, which are very much part of the Spanish culture.

There was such a contrast when we finally flew her home. The family felt like no one among us could stay down there forever with her, and my son is five hours away running a hotel. We medevacked her home, and of course, the side effect of that is that there is more pressure on the brain. So there is more inflammation again. But once she's in the hospital here, they are saying to us immediately, in front of my mother, which I made sure they never did again, "Well, from everything you said we thought she was going to be much more aware than she is," and blah, blah, blah.

Instead of celebrating what was there, they were already telling us what wasn't. They were focusing on what wasn't instead of what was.

It was like night and day. And you know what? I saw it in my mother's demeanor. That's when she finally started accepting that this was probably the end. And, you know, she ended up with a bedsore. Most of the time when people have these things, they actually die of the secondary infections that they get, like pneumonia or bedsores or bacterial infections. And that's basically what started happening. I wanted her to go home. But my dad didn't want that.

This is something I've had to forgive my dad for, because I think he has his own reality and I have mine, which is true for all of us, isn't it? But I asked him in the hall at the hospital, "Dad, if we're going to do the respite route, why don't we take care of Mom at home?" I said, "We could get VNA," which is Vermont Nurses Association, "to help staff it. And there are enough of us, and we'll help you with it."

But he said to me, "No. They're not going to give us enough help. I couldn't handle that."

I said, "Well, let's look into it. There's nothing wrong with looking into it."

Then he looked at me, and he said, "Well, if you want her you can have her," just like that.

I just looked at him and I said – this is me – I said, "You mean Mom's not welcome back in her own home?" And he looked at me and he started getting red – his blood pressure rose and I could see it. He got red from the neck all the way up and then he got blotchy at the top of his head.

Then he said to me, "Why don't you grow up?" This is something you would say to a 9-year-old kid or a 5-year-old kid or a teenager, right? But to your 63-year-old daughter? So I didn't say anything, because if I said something it wouldn't have been the most loving thing I could have said. So I did one of my basketball pivot steps as fast as I could, and I went right back into my mother's hospital room and started stroking her so I could calm down. Because this was about her. It was not about my father, it was not about me; it was about her. And I have to say, that was my focus through this whole thing.

I looked at it this way: this might be the last time I have with my mom, and what I want to do no matter what the decision is, is to do what's right for her. It has nothing to do with my needs, it has nothing to do with my siblings' needs, and it has nothing to do with my father's needs. This is about my mother.

And that was always my focus. And that's what helped me make the decisions I needed to make. She ended up going into the respite house, and I think the reason my mother stayed alive so long, to tell you the truth, is that she wanted to come home. She was in Costa Rica when this happened. She wanted to be in her home, where they have these antique clocks that chime and all of these things that would let her know she was home. And so my one regret is that my father did not have the constitution or the strength or the lack of fear to be able to deal with my mother passing in her own home.

I can't know what it's like to be him. Maybe he felt it would have wrecked that house for him forever. I don't know. I'm trying to be as forgiving and loving as I can, but it's the one thing I think my mother would have wanted that he was unwilling to give her after 67 years of marriage.

I suppose she understood him. She probably waited for me to be gone sometimes in the hospital. Us women. Isn't this the theme we're talking about here, about us women and how we're so concerned about everyone else's needs? I'm thinking I should be there and she's thinking I shouldn't be there, right?

There's a minor point about the respite home that still bothers me. When I was there with her, everyone was talking about, "What a beautiful place for your mother to be," and there were rabbits and birds and all of these things. But the way my mother was laying, there's no way she could have seen the place. And I'm thinking, this is for us, it's not for her. Because my focus is always about my mom. She can't see any of this stuff in this hospital bed. This is for all of us, to feel my mother is in a good place. But she probably did feel the energy of all those beautiful things around her.

Still, I kept thinking she should be home among those things she would have known and felt, instead of feeling like she's in a hotel room kind of place.

Something else that is still very powerful in my mind a year later, because now we've gone through the one year anniversary of all of these events, is about when she decided to go. I remember the night before her birthday in the respite home, and I could tell that things were getting tougher for her. I said, "You know Mom, you can do what's right for you, and we'll all know and feel grateful for everything we've already had from you. But if you decide that you want to do this, if you wait till after midnight, you'll live to be 89." I said, "It's up to you. You do what's right, but I just thought I'd remind you."

The next day we had a little party – all the family was there for her birthday, and we had a cake in her room. She passed away around 9 o'clock at night. I'm sure she was thinking it's time for my sister, who came over from across the lake, and for everyone else to go home before it's too dark. But the thing that was the most impactful – that I'll continue to live with forever – was that when it was time for her to go – and you could tell by her breathing – we were all with her. And I was kind of massaging her arm and she gave me 100 percent eye contact and I was starting to talk her through it. My father came into the room at that point, and she looked at him for a little bit and then locked right back into my eyes. I was the one that talked her through.

One of my brothers died 23 years ago, one of her twins. Her babies were the twins. So I was saying to her, "Mom, Michael is waiting for you. We've had you for a real long time. And Michael's there and he can't wait to see you again. And you know what Michael's like. You better be ready." Michael lived in New Orleans, and he took my mother to Mardi Gras, and brought her to Saks Fifth Avenue. He dressed her in gowns, he got her jewels, and she went to the ball with him. I said, "He died when he was 31. He was full of fun." So I said to her, "Mom, Michael is waiting. You better be ready. You know all the fun you're going to have with him."

So we were talking about things like that and we were saying, "You've taught us how to live a life, and we're certainly going to miss you. But if we can't do it without you now, there's something wrong with us. So you've got to do what's right for you."

And I was saying all this stuff with everyone around her. It's funny how when everyone is around a death bed, every one has a different role. My sister was doing the blood pressure thing, checking her pulse; and so was my niece. And I just was heart to heart with my mom. So her eyes never left my face until her last breath.

But the one thing I did that I know made it easier for her – that I feel really good about – was connecting her with my brother Raymond. He had just left to go back to Chicago when she was put in the respite house, because it could have been weeks until the end. We didn't know how long. He had to get back to his job. So I called Raymond and I said, "Raymond, you need to talk to Mom. I'm going to put the cell phone right by her ear, because you're the only one that's not here."

Raymond is the other twin, and those were her babies. And he was the one she was the closest to, because he stayed with her the longest as a young adult before he left home. I put Raymond on the phone with her, and at one point I realized that the phone was dead. While I was talking to my mom I was holding the phone by her ear, and I realized the phone was dead, so I called him back. I said, "Raymond, where are you?"

He said, "I told her everything I needed to say and I told her I'd call her back in an hour."

I said, "Raymond, she's not gonna be here in an hour," and then he started to cry.

He said, "Well what do I say to her?" I said, "I don't care what you say to her. She needs to hear your voice and you need to know this is the last time you're going to be talking to your mom. And I'll let you know when she's no longer there." And so he talked to her for another 15 minutes on the cell phone. She had me with eye contact and with what I was saying to her softly, and she had him in her ear, and that's how she went.

And then afterwards, my new sister-in-law – my other brother divorced in his 60s – came up to me and said, "You made your mother's path so easy. You walked her right through it." She was the only one that acknowledged that role that I had, but I'm sure that everyone else noticed it. It was interesting: Leave it to another woman who has nothing to do with the family history and all the family emotions to be the one to let me know how important I had been.

As for my role afterwards, well, we had decided we were going to do a memorial service. My mother wanted to be cremated. There were family issues that my mother had always managed for us before, you know – all the personalities and stuff. And now she's gone.

So now again the whole thing for me is around what's right for Mom. That made it really easy. I have always been the one with the deepest pockets when it came to finances. So the way I got to make sure the service was about my mom and not about everyone else's agendas, and got to keep it as peaceful and about her as I could, was to pick up the cost for everything. It worked out to be two and two. I have a sister and another brother, but my brother Raymond and I are more in sync. So every time someone wanted to do something that we felt was not going to be in Mom's best interest for the service, I would say, "Well, anyone who wants to pitch in, can help out in any way they'd like." And they'd back down. So I said, "I'm doing this for Mom and this is going to be done the way she would like it, and I'm just going to pick up the whole tab," because I knew I would be able to do it that way. They didn't want to pay for their control.

I'm a good strategist.

After the service, it was no longer about my mom anymore. I certainly want to be there for my dad in the way that he would like us to be there, but that's very different from how my mom would have wanted. My father is very independent. He hates to be accountable. Like if you said, "Dad, you want to come over for dinner tonight? I'm having it at 7 and I'm having so and so come. Can you join us?" he'd say, "Well, I'll see."

His whole idea is that something better might come up between now and then. It used to drive my mother nuts. I think I came to know with my father that independence is important, not pinning him down is important, and I have to love him a different way. And as much as I have a history with him that I cherish and so many good traits that have come from him, my mother was the heart of the family.

So my legacy now is to continue being effective in a dysfunctional family, coming from her love – without these being my children. That's a tough role. Now, they have actually made it easy for me, because my sister and my brother understand that we don't speak the same language. They're more fundamentalist in their attitude. I've always been very creative and artistic. And I come from fewer rules than they do and less judgment, and I'd like to continue being that way. So it's just a difference in the way they function and the way I function.

My brother Raymond and I talk often about how some of us take after our mother and some of us take after our father. My father was raised in a shame-based family. He is the most successful of the ten children, and he came the furthest away from that background because of my mother's love. He was smart enough to pick the right person for himself, who helped to detox the influences that he had had, and he was a very bright man and high-achieving man. But we kind of chuckle, Raymond and I, because we're even built similarly; our dad's tall, but we're both small-boned. We feel like we took after our mother and my other brother and sister took after my father – they're even built differently. We just know there was a kind of division in my family in the gene pool as far as our emotional well-being. There's not a lot of connection. When they're around me, I can be as loving as I can be, but I'm not going to be something I'm not.

So our family can be at an event and be very physically present and be nice to one another to one another's faces, but when push comes to shove there are things that are being said when we're not there. I have only one way of being, and that's truthful. I certainly don't want to say anything hurtful, but I'm not going to say anything that's not the truth either. So they don't spend a lot of time around me and it works fine, because I have this beautiful family, my friends, and a brother who comes from the same place as me, and my father certainly appreciates me a lot. I've also developed my Nikken family and friends – you can't choose your family but you can choose your friends – and some of those friends whom I originally met through my business have been with me for so long that they're more like family. With my sister, unfortunately, I certainly still care about her, but she's not someone that really speaks my language anymore.

So since my mom's death, my role has been limited in the family, except for a promise I made to my mom, as I think my brother did also. My mother was very religious and spiritual. I think she is one of the few people who are both, and she got a lot of solace, believe it or not, from the Catholic Church, which has been generally patriarchal. But the monsignor who was my mother's really good friend at the cathedral here in Burlington was not patriarchal, and my mother got all the benefits of a healthy religious life in her parish. She was considered a leader and was acknowledged by the parish. She gave communion, she was one of the people who were very, very involved in the parish, and they recognized her and made her feel successful outside of her beautiful role in our family and also outside of the business that she and my father created together. My brother's promise to my mom was that he would go back to church on Sunday, because it was a way to be with my mom, and it's something my mother would have loved to see.

And my promise to my mother was that I would always take care of my brother Raymond. He's ten years younger than me and he's my mother's baby. So what I take very seriously is Raymond's well-being. And Raymond knows that. I told him I made that promise. I even told my father I made that promise. I didn't say to my mother, "I'll take care of Dad." It's not like I don't want to help with my dad, but I knew what was meaningful to my mom and as I've said, for me it was about her.

So that's really been what I feel.

Then another piece is that each generation leaves in us their story; that's what we're trying to immortalize with this book, and I so appreciate it. But each generation has passed on to us the stories we have of them and our demeanor and way of life which they helped create in us. And now that I'm in my mother's role with a grandchild coming, I'm so aware of what my role is and my legacy. It's to continue the spirit of love which my mother just did so intuitively, and to do it in a way that is me but at the same time honors her.

It's really interesting that my son actually chose a woman this time around that's so much like his grandmother. It's going to be very interesting to watch, and I actually even shared that observation with them. My son has a very strong personality. Both my husband and I have unique, strong personalities and we have different ways of exhibiting them. He's very introverted and I'm extroverted, but we both know what we stand for. And so we raised this one child who's come from two strong parents who are different, and he's very strong himself, because we treated him as an equal as he became older and he always had a part in our decision-making.

He has this wonderful Spanish woman in his life, and obviously she's more from a strong ethnic background, like my mother, who was French-Canadian. She's coming from this same love and support that my mother always gave to us her children, and to my father.

I said to my son JT, "You have a chance to rewrite the marriage you saw with Papa and Nana." I said, "You saw that Nana didn't voice her opinion as much as she needed to and had other ways of getting her needs fulfilled other than having the conversations I'm sure you're going to want to have with Katerine. And you saw that Papa often times didn't understand that he was overpowering her energy in that marriage." I went on, "You've chosen someone closer to Nana, and your personality is a warmer version of your grandfather. So do you think you can rewrite what you've seen and heard, watching them and their marriage, and rewrite it with a better script?" That's the conversation we've had.

And now JT and his wife are just about to have their first child. That's the legacy. It's not only the legacy that my mother expressed in the life she led herself as an individual, but it's also the legacy that she shared with us as one successful way of being a woman in a family setting. I said to JT, "There are so many successful ways of being a woman in a family setting, but it's all right to choose your grandmother's energy in your own wife, since you're so attracted to that energy. Just be aware of the journey that you watched with your grandparents and what kind of male you want to be in that environment."

So the teaching continues, and there's going to be a grandchild that's going to get exposed to that energy, that legacy. Fortunately, I have the kind of relationship with my son that we can talk this way and he gets it.

I do need to learn Spanish though, because JT's wife doesn't speak English very well.

I've shared the things that I felt I needed to say, things I'm probably sharing for my own purposes.

I definitely have little moments which remind me of my mom, now that a year has past. There are moments that Raymond and I talk about a lot. One of them happened on the day of her birthday. Raymond was in Chicago and was getting something out of his car. What does he see? Something which has obviously been there for close to a year – the card that was given out at her memorial service, with the poem and her dates. And he said, "What are the odds of my finding this on the anniversary of her birthday and of her death?" He said, "That was Mom just saying hi, you know."

And there have been other such moments for me, but the thing that comes to my mind right now that I want to share is that I have a yard full of birds which I like to entice to come near. Many times I'll be thinking of my mom, and just then there will be a cardinal that will come and start singing in my yard. And my mother had a thing for cardinals! We always gave her cardinal cards and cardinal Christmas ornaments. And she had cardinals in her yard. Ever since my mother's death, I have two to three times more cardinals in my yard.

It's her way of reminding me of her, not that I need that many reminders1 We just passed my first Mother's Day without my mom and as you know my mother was born and then died around Mother's Day, since both were May 13th. Someone said to me this Mother's Day, "I'm thinking of you. It must be hard." And, you know, it wasn't hard, because those aren't the times that are hard. The times that are hard for me are when something wonderful has happened to me, and I just need to call my mom and tell her about it. And I go to do it and I realize I can't.

Another thing that has happened is that there has been a lot of forward movement in my Nikken business. My brother took over my mother's Nikken business, and I think she's orchestrating things from above.

The business she had with my dad they sold many, many years ago, when my father was 55. They built the business together, but my father ran it and my mother was the supporter. I have support in me, but I've got some of my dad. I'm not just the supporter; I'm also the orchestrator.

My mother's role definitely influenced me in my career path. From the time I was very young I knew – and I don't know how I knew, but once I understood it I realized that I've always felt this way from a very young age – that my path, my karmic path, was to take the best of what it meant to be a man, and add it to being a woman. Don't forget, I came from a Quebecois, that is, French-Canadian, environment, both mother and father, with a very patriarchal Catholic upbringing. And what I saw was that the men were the doers as far as the kind of doing that brings home the money, and the women were the lovers and the ones who kept the family fires going. They were the relationship guiders. The men seemed like they had more flexibility in their schedule and were able to do more fun things that had to do with achieving, and women did the things that everyone appreciated but sometimes didn't acknowledge until way later in life.

So I knew that I wanted to get the best of both worlds. I knew it from the beginning, and I actually used to have a symbol for it, because I wore the Infinity necklace which Nikken sold for a while. I have the male and the female energy, because I didn't want to lose all the wonderful things that it meant to be a woman, all that nurturing and giving and loving. And I wanted to have the fun and achievements that come from being a man in the culture I was raised in. So from a very young age, my mother encouraged that side of me, and even my father did in his own way. He was very proud of my achievements. But I didn't ever want it to be at the cost of what it meant to be a woman.

So I think the person my mother was has instructed me and encouraged me to be everything she was, but also to take on some of the things that I think made her so proud of who I was. There was never anything I did that she didn't support. I competed in body building, and she went to every one of my shows up to age 51. I was Mrs. Vermont after my first show, and they asked me to be in a pageant to represent Vermont nationally, so I went to Plano, Texas to do it. Both my parents were sitting in the audience, just as if I was 13 and they were going to one of my recitals.

I think that later in life my mother lived vicariously through my life. She participated in everything I did, she helped take the money at my executive lunches, and she became a Silver consultant in the Nikken structure. She just loved being kind of my sidekick.

She continued supporting the best in all of us right till the very end. She's going to be dearly, dearly missed, and I'll never be her, but there are pieces of me that are there because of her.

I don't know if there is more of her in me now since her death, but I'm more aware of it. I have an open home like she did, and anyone who comes in is always made to feel welcome. It's a drop-by place, and the more the merrier. All those things came from my mother's joyous Quebecois background, part of that culture. I'm certainly aware that I don't want to waste the time I have here, and I certainly want to create a legacy of something meaningful, like she did.

My mother came from a retail family and my father came from an agrarian family. And you can see the difference. One was more introverted and the other one is out there with people.

I remember when my mother lost her mother. And I remember it was really hard on my mom. She was one of thirteen children, actually fifteen children but two died young. Mothers are very important things in our lives. My mother was raised by a mother that knew how to love. That's why my mother was so loving. And fortunately for me, I had a mother like that.

I remember her mother's death being hard for her, but my mother had five children to be there for her. I think I was away for most of that time, away at college I think, when it happened. My mother and I had a few conversations around that time, but I don't have strong memories of them. I came home for the funeral and things, but the day-to-day stuff that you run into when your mom is gone I wasn't around for.

Then when my mom died, I was there with her, and I was the only direct family member, other than my father and my son, who was there with her for the whole process which started in Costa Rica. So it's like one of those things where the impression that I have of my mother's death is probably going to be stronger than anyone's just because I was there through the whole thing.

So she graced me with that, didn't she?

The funny thing is that I was the more positive one in my mother's life and I made her feel what she was capable of doing instead of limiting her. My sister was the one that took on the medical role with her, but she was more traditional. She was a nurse. I think if my mother had involved me more – she always thought I was so busy – with what was happening for her at the end, there might have been some different outcomes. I think my mother always pretended with me that everything was okay, because she wanted to do all the fun things with me, like going to Costa Rica.

If I'm surprised about anything in this time since she's been gone, it's how I've managed to go on without this amazing woman in my life. I expected to feel more nonfunctional, and the thing is I'm functioning fine, but I don't know what I've done in that process to make that possible. That's something still to be uncovered. With everything I went through in those last days, with focusing entirely on my mom, because that to me is what you do, and with all of that when she was still around, I had little time to think of myself.

You must focus on them when they're here. And so as long as she was here, she was my priority. And when she wasn't here, then I had to pick up the pieces that were left after all of that focus. What ended up happening to me is I ended up having an under-functioning thyroid, which I haven't had before, as far as I know. The thyroid represents your voice. So I wonder, did I not express enough of everything I needed to express, so now my thyroid is showing me that it's having an issue? I don't know. Maybe this strength that I have is misused in some way, I don't know. Maybe I'm not honoring all the sadness. Maybe I'm not doing all of the deep work I need to do, but I know I'll do it in my own time frame, and I know I have been doing it to some extent, and I will continue to do it. The thyroid connection is interesting to me.

My naturopathic doctor said that she feels this is a short term thing for me. She said, "This is how your body expressed the trauma that you've had this year with all you went through when you were being superwoman. And this is how your body is letting you know that it's time for you to do some things a little differently. I think that this will be short-lived in you, that you'll probably only need to take something to support your thyroid for about year." It's kind of like priming the pump again.

I think I keep going and going and going and stop thinking about it. These are the things that make us stop and learn from the things we do and don't do and learn where to find balance.

For other women going through this process, I guess my theme, and the way I was able to handle it, is my question: I said to myself the whole time, "What would Mother want?" All the time. So it wasn't about what I might have wanted to do or what anyone else had wanted to do or what my father wanted to do. I felt that the last thing I could do for my mom is to think for her when she couldn't express for herself. And having been so close to my mom, I think that was the thing that got me through. It was to say, "What would Mom want?" And then focus all my attention on what Mom would want. And that gave me some sanity.

That's the one thing that I would advise to anyone. Just focus that way. If you come from that and you keep saying that, the rest of the family has to respect that, because there's tons of stuff that happens within in the rest of the family. Everyone manages all those things differently. But that's how I used to always come back; I'd always come back to that. People would see that I wasn't doing this for me – it wasn't them against me – it was them against what I knew were Mother's wishes.

God could not be everywhere and therefore he made mothers.
JEWISH PROVERB

CHAPTER 9

YOUR VOYAGE FROM TRAGEDY TO TRIUMPH: THE SEVEN T'S

Your pain is real and important and needs your attention and energy. Even though your mother is released from her final suffering or lived a great life surrounded by love or otherwise died after a good life, your side of the equation is equally important.

Our religious traditions describe various images of what happens after death. You may subscribe to any of these or others. They may include a transition to a new life free of tears; a reunion with a deceased husband or with parents who went before or a beloved cousin, friend, sibling or even child; or the fulfillment of your mother's hopes for enjoying the presence of her divine maker. It seems that the finality of death takes the exact nature of her existence after death out of our hands. We may pray that she has everything she wanted, but there is nothing much else we can do except what we do now here to make her legacy real and true.

Philosophically, we may consider that she is now one with the energies of the universe, or her soul is now informing our own, guiding us in a new way, perhaps imperceptible to us but sometimes a felt presence or a flash of energy. Perhaps she is to be reborn.

Your belief system is yours alone

But it is important that you know what it is or take the time to find out. It will be an important source of comfort now and throughout your life.

For myself, I didn't dwell on any particular doctrine about heaven or divine judgment or the continuity of consciousness or identity. I like to think that my departed mother now knows all and is content with her life as she lived it. I like to picture her smiling at it all, content at how all the struggles, misunderstandings, worries, and pain were far outweighed by the laughter, the triumphs, the love, and the joy. That is the way she lived her life. I like to think of her laughing, along with my father, at all the daily concerns with which we fill our lives and sending good vibes to me to remind me to laugh as I go along, as they used to, to keep things in perspective, and to value love above all.

Psychologically, experts pontificate on how long healthy mourning lasts. Every culture in the past has had different traditions, but all have recognized the necessity of mourning. Since the triumph of rationality in Western culture, much of this has disappeared. Being scientifically disposed, we have done away with many rituals and outward signs of mourning. Public lamentation has been replaced by private moments of dread and aloneness. We have internalized our feelings and even feel embarrassed to show public mourning which might make others uncomfortable.

Now that we all are presumed to have jobs and careers, the death of an ailing parent is presumed to allow us to get back to focusing on our work. We may have young children still or kids in college, or grown children with their own children. In any case, we have work and family to get back to ASAP. The grief can be handled at home, we think. If it drags on, or turns into some kind of depression, sleeplessness, change in appetite, or anxiety, we can simply medicate it. Science now knows, the TV ads tell us, how to reduce any unwanted feelings, at least for a time, while we are still "processing" the loss.

But as Meghan O'Rourke said in the interview mentioned earlier about her book *The Long Goodbye,* about her mother's death with cancer when O'Rourke was 30, ""Loss isn't science; it's a human reckoning. In my case, it means I have to reckon every day with my mother's absence."

Inadequate social mourning

Joyce Carol Oates pointed out in that same interview how there is a certain irony in public ritual – there is "Too much that is impersonal in a way to deflect the horror of the specific unique death." She noted also that the more ancient unrestrained outpourings of grief, with "widows tearing their hair and rending their garments," could "help express grief's physical intensity – without the mourner having to be embarrassed."

The front we present to others of how we are dealing with the loss and the way we feel in private may be entirely different things. When my father died, I spent a great deal of time being strong for my mother and helping her avoid falling into a fatal slump, while meanwhile being strong as a mother for my then small children and trying to deal with all that goes on when a parent dies. But inside, I lost my appetite and my husband did the cooking in my stead for weeks. And I invited a friend who was a minister to hold a private service just for me, my family, and a cousin with whom I felt I could let my hair down, or rather, start "tearing my hair" would be more like it.

Each of us is individual in the way we separate our public and private grief. But it is important that we know both exist and both are normal and to be expected, by us, our loved ones, and the society at large.

In that same rare article about grief, Oates is in the generation previous to ours and O'Rourke is in the generation after ours. Oates quoted from her book, *A Widow's Story*, saying that the bottom line is, "To find a way, however desperate, to keep yourself alive." How many of those around us can possibly appreciate how that feels if they haven't lost anyone really close?

The scandal sheets on the racks at the checkout lines in the supermarket love to show horrible pictures of people whom we normally recognize and idolize for their beauty and fame, when they are in mourning for a loss of some kind. Do we look like that?

Do we feel like that? What about how in many ancient cultures it was assumed you would mourn for at least a year? In Jewish tradition mirrors were turned to the wall so that wailing and weeping would not embarrass the mourners. And the wearing of black until recently was a way to put people on notice that you needed a bit more sensitive treatment than the next guy because you were dealing with personal loss.

Do you remember the scenes of mourning for Southern Bell Scarlet O'Hara in the film *Gone with the Wind*? She didn't want to wear black for very long after her first husband died in the Civil War. She had only married him to be near his brother-in-law. Then when her mother died, she was devastated, but she couldn't even take time to mourn, because she had to take leadership of her family and household in the aftermath of the war. When faced with the death of her child, she knew nothing mattered but the people around her and when her sister-in-law died, her life changed completely. What a horrible time when families were torn apart by civil war, and epidemics and death were an everyday matter.

We are indeed fortunate that we had our mothers so long, that they died at a respectable age, and that they even came to know their grandchildren and often even great-grandchildren. Popular wisdom tells us that deaths which happen in the normal order should not upset the cart too much. It is a tragedy when a young child loses a parent or a parent loses a child. These are out of the natural order. But a mother or grandmother in her 50s or 60s whose mother dies in her 70s, 80s, or 90s should be satisfied that she had her around so long and should undoubtedly have seen it coming. We feel for the daughter who must care-take her ailing mother for any significant length of time, but when the end comes, we are supposed to welcome it as a blessing. She is out of pain. She has lived a good life. She loved her children and grandchildren. All is well.

But we the daughter-mothers left standing don't feel that way. Yes, we are in control, we knew it was coming, we can manage, we can keep on keeping on, we will fulfill our duties to our families, and so on. But that's all a bit irrelevant to what is going on for us, inside us.

A good case can be made for an even deeper sense of emptiness the longer our mothers have been with us. Perhaps the most famous mother to daughter-mother relationship in our lifetime has been Queen Elizabeth II and the Queen Mother. Queen Elizabeth assumed the British throne in 1952 at the age of twenty five. Her Queen Mother passed away in March of 2002, a few months before her 102nd birthday. Though royal grief is largely kept private, it would be wrong to think that the Queen's grief was any less because her mother lived so wonderfully long. Yet the Queen had to go on with her life, keeping her households, working a lifelong career as queen which she never chose for herself, and being a mother and grandmother all along as well. She must have missed her mother deeply at the wedding of Will and Kate which the whole world was watching.

The future offers questions as big as those about the past

No matter what our beliefs about what happens when we die, it is the continuity of life which tends to occupy our thoughts. What and where our mothers are now is not as great a preoccupation as one might think. Rather, our thoughts focus more on what her life meant and means now and how we will choose to play out her legacy. Your feelings are gifts to grace the stage of your mind. Watch them come and go and interact and a beautiful story can emerge.

Five stages of grief were identified by Elizabeth Kubler-Ross over 40 years ago, after she interviewed hundreds of people who were facing their own deaths. Her ground-breaking book was called *On Death and Dying.* Since then these five stages have helped to make sense of almost any kind of loss and the mourning process we go through, from losing a loved one to losing a job or even to giving up an addictive behavior.

These stages she named Denial, Anger, Bargaining, Depression, and Acceptance. Kubler-Ross was careful to point out that not everyone experiences all five stages and that they do not always occur in any particular order. In addition those grieving often vacillate between the various stages and also can sometimes get stuck in one stage with little recourse unless they seek help. Some more recent research has challenged these categories, but I have found in my counseling practice that they serve admirably to help characterize the different reactions we can have to loss, and they serve well to help you to focus on your feelings when as a mother yourself you feel for your mother's feelings in dying as well as for your own.

The danger of not letting the grieving take its course is that we will get stuck in one of the earlier stages and any number of unwanted effects can occur. So let's review the stages in the particular context of the loss of our mothers and then continue on with the powerful stories you will read in the remainder of *Mothers Losing Mothers*.

Because Kubler-Ross's categories ended with the death of the person because they were coming to grips with their own death, acceptance was the last stage. She did not address any stages which may come after death. There may be more, as reported by people who have clinically died and then been returned to life. For example, on my weekly radio program *Family First*,[9] Dean Braxton told his story of being clinically dead for over an hour and a half, as verified by the doctors who treated him and his medical records. Upon his return to life, Braxton reported a definite awareness beyond his death of all-encompassing love and fulfillment. He tells his story in his book *In Heaven Experiencing the Throne of God*.[10]

Because we live past our mother's death, I believe there are stages beyond acceptance for us who continue living. So I suggest seven stages, the first five paralleling the familiar five stages with two new ones added. I call these stages the Seven T's.

Tragedy

The first stage is the stage of Denial. In the context of losing your mother, it is when hope fails you and you realize that the end of

---

[9] *Family First* airs live on Fridays at 1PM Pacific/ 3PM Central/ 4PM Eastern, on the VoiceAmerica Health & Wellness Channel. To access the show, log on at http://www.voiceamericahealth.com. All shows are available in Randy Rolfe's Content Library on The VoiceAmerica Health & Wellness Channel for on-demand and podcast download, http://www.voiceamericahealth.com.
[10] Dean Braxton, *In Heaven Experiencing the Throne of God* (Maitland, FL: Xulon Press, 2009).

your mother's life is near. It feels tragic no matter how long a life she has lived. Tragedy happens when someone high, in whatever dimension, has a severe fall. For our mothers, who are so important to us, their death feels tragic. As your hope begins to fade and your efforts become more futile to maintain your hope and hers that this current health challenge will pass as perhaps others have, you tend to deny that the end could be coming, and in the end, that it has really come. Our loss is tragic and we react as one would to a tragedy. When this moment hit me in the hospital with my mother, I was moved to call a friend and mentor who had always been there for me in my business endeavors. She patiently heard my story and bolstered my courage by sharing a bit of her story of losing her mother. Hearing an outside voice from someone who understood gave me the strength to come out of denial and know that I would survive this tragedy.

Our first reaction to deny the reality of the tragedy is actually a valuable adaptive response to a shock to our system and should not be cause for embarrassment or self-doubt. Among American soldiers fighting in Iraq and Afghanistan in recent years, it was discovered that it was counterproductive and even dangerous to try to get soldiers to talk about their most traumatic experiences too soon after the event. Unfortunately we have had to learn more in recent years about post-traumatic stress disorder, or what used to be called battle fatigue. Much progress has been made with talk therapy since previous wars. But psychologists working with soldiers who had suffered horrible experiences found that the soldiers did better if they were not cajoled into sharing their feelings before they were ready.

This sounds like they are experiencing the first stage of grieving, the stage of denial. Forcing someone out of this self-protective stage can be damaging, the counselors found. The brain simply blocks out the traumatic experience in an effort to protect the vital functions of the body and the brain. In mourning the loss of our mother, this can feel internally like numbness, paralysis, not being able to cry, not being able to focus, or not wanting to move. It may look externally like absolutely nothing happened; we simply go about our business.

If we get stuck in this stage, we may face a serious inability to relate to life and to feel much of anything anymore. Instead we need to accept that we want to pretend it didn't happen and let that numbness and resistance pass.

Torment

In the second stage, the stage of Anger, which I will call Torment, we torment ourselves with the question, why couldn't it be different? The stage of anger serves the purpose of moving us towards the realization that a major life event has occurred. It is natural to feel anger at our mother for leaving, anger at our loved ones for not getting how grieved we feel, anger at the medical team, anger at fate or God, and anger at ourselves for not having done more or been able to do more. I felt lots of anger and let its wave break over me. I felt the doctors had done too little and too much. I was angry I did not know what to say when I had so often been able to say the right thing at the right time as a counselor and even as a daughter and a mother. I was angry at modern end-of-life practices, thinking my mother would have rather been at home if the doctors had been clear that the end was inevitable.

I knew to just go ahead and feel my anger because of what a wise mentor of mine told me years ago. He said that anger is an emotion which comes when we think we should have been able to control more than we actually could, and it forces us to face the limits of our power and to eventually appreciate what power we do have. Anger can also move us to self-pity. Why couldn't we control the situation? What more could we have done, or our mother have done, or the doctors have done, or God have done, to prevent this loss?

Anger at the death of my mother was real. I helped to keep her healthy with my encouragement, my love, and my nutrition advice. I helped her to find good doctors and helped her to comply with their good advice. I tried to make her confident and comfortable enough to continue what she loved most – her travel and her gardening and her dedication to family and friends. I tried to engage her with her children and grandchildren so she would see how much they loved having her in their lives.

I did all these things. But I eventually discovered that I had no control of how and when she would go. Of course I felt anger. I still have to remind myself that I did not have control over these things. I only could help and do what I could do. Things happen in their own way.

If you get stuck with your natural anger, you can become irritable, anxious, aggressive, nervous, fearful, and more likely to overreact to others' transgressions. It is important when you are in this stage to warn your loved ones that you may be over-emotional or lash out unexpectedly. Be quick to apologize and explain that it is not about them but rather about you. Let them know you expect it to change with time.

If you accept your angry feelings and your urge to pin blame, to find someone or something responsible for your pain, it will be easier to move on. When feelings are accepted as feelings and not the absolute truth of the matter, another feeling will soon replace them.

Transition

The next stage is the Bargaining stage, what I call Transition, like the transition stage in childbirth. We think we can manage the situation, we bargain with those around us and with God to end the suffering. Are we trying to manage our pain? It doesn't work, we eventually discover. When we try to bargain away our pain, we seek help from church guides, spiritual mentors, doctors, the Internet, books, meditations, new activities, old activities, busyness, and more, to mollify our sadness.

This is a fascinating stage which is hard to recognize so it's helpful to know that it's a natural part of dealing with an event beyond your control. I certainly tried to stay busy, to relax, to pray, to remember good times, to get all the details from the doctors and hospice care workers, to do research, to replay last words, and so on, all in an effort to bring more peace and understanding to the situation. But the fact is still there. An event beyond my control had turned my life upside down, even if only for a limited time.

You figure out ways that you can deal with the loss by changing yourself or your circumstances or getting others to make up for the loss. You may try to make bargains with God to stop the hurt or to bargain with your husband, your children, your siblings, or others to take on more of the pain to try to ease your own. We think, if we stay occupied, if we think positive thoughts, if we focus on supporting others, if we pray really hard, if we build a shrine, or any number of other plans, our pain will be less.

Again these natural defenses and maneuvers can help move us towards a resolution to our pain, but they do not reduce the actual impact of this potentially life-changing event. The big question remains of how do you survive and thrive as a mature human woman when you have seen the woman who bore you disappear from this earth.

This too is not a place to stay stuck. It starts to look and feel like a kind of manipulation of feelings and behaviors to avoid dealing with the real changes that have happened without your permission and beyond your control.

Trial

The fourth stage, Depression or Despair, is what I call the Trial in the context of the loss of your mother. We ask ourselves, is there truly no rest for the weary? We have worn ourselves out trying to manipulate and avoid feeling our pain. In this stage, we either give up in a despairing way, or we surrender to what is, and try to bootstrap our way to another state of mind. This moment hit me one day shortly after my mother's death when I was swimming. I have already shared this story with you.

Again this depression and despair is a natural reaction to this traumatic event. Depression often involves suppression of emotion. It is normal to try to suppress your emotional suffering, perhaps out of fear of its intensity, perhaps because we feel we shouldn't feel this way, or perhaps because we see no way out – that it will not end if we let ourselves experience it. If it is not suppressed, it may well look like despair and that is scary. We might rather stay depressed.

It is healthy, just a part of the mourning process, to sense this low point and to surrender to a power greater than ourselves and experience our feelings, for when we do so, ironically, they are then free to change. Accepting our defeat allows us to surrender and receive guidance on how to move beyond this bottom to higher ground.

Tranquility

The fifth classic stage of mourning, the stage of Acceptance, I call Tranquility. It's when we finally let go. We are letting go, but of what? We are taking our first steps on a path towards acceptance of the event. We are letting go of our hopes, anger, self-manipulations, and despair to put one foot in front of the other on a new path. The idea of acceptance can feel very scary and we naturally resist its implications for our mothers and ourselves. We must do so even for our children, since we have to accept that even if we and they are fortunate in life and live out or exceed our expected lifespan, we and they will be going through a similar experience together.

We come to where we must accept the sadness. By now you have come to terms with the actual fact of the loss, that it just is and there is nothing you can do to undo it. Your brain is now ready to try to move forward, to assess your new situation, however that looks to you, and to plot a fresh course. It is an opportunity to look around you and decide, what now?

Being stuck at this stage is less dangerous than the previous ones, but accepting the reality of the loss doesn't give you the energy to move on. Whatever you need to do to let your mother in, to integrate what she is to you into your being, will allow you to move beyond acceptance to a kind of serenity where, as a good friend said about losing his father, "You never get over it, you just learn to live with it."

Transformation

After these five stages, occurring in whatever order and feedback loop happen for you, you may finally come to feel transformed. For people facing their own death, as in the studies done by Kubler-Ross, the last stage was the stage Acceptance, accepting that death was coming. For many of us we recognize that our mothers did reach that stage of Acceptance, and a sense of Tranquility did seem to come over them. Many did not speak after a certain point, once they had said goodbye to us.

But for us who remain here, Tranquility is not enough to sustain us through our lives as mother, wife/lover, woman, and person in our community, for what we hope will be several more decades. So I have added two more stages.

One feeling leads to another as long as we are alive and as long as we let it happen, believing in ourselves. So if we let the feelings of the Tranquility stage settle in a bit, we may begin to sense a new stage of Transformation. Feelings may include appreciation and gratitude, a sense of relief, a new energy pulling us to explore, to learn, to teach, or to celebrate. We may feel we are reaching a new level of awareness, having experienced a once in a lifetime transformation of perhaps the most powerful relationship in our lives, our bond with our mother.

Allowing ourselves to be tranquil, to experience that sense of peace and surrender, tends to be transformative, as spiritual teachers have claimed throughout history. If you give the necessary time and energy to your personal process, a new momentum will in all likelihood take hold. Your mother's life is a gift, to be gratefully received and celebrated through your own life that she gave you. You may discover that you are part of a stupendous process of creation and re-creation beyond your control but beautiful and awesome to behold.

After all, becoming a mother is the most direct representation of the cosmic creative process that we as humans are witness to and we neglect its impact at our peril. Instead we can remain humble in our appreciation of our motherly power, while at the same time expressing in our daily life the transformative legacy which one human generation passes on to the next and the next.

Triumph

When you are able to fully accept the gifts your mother left you, physical, intellectual, emotional, spiritual, and social, these cannot help but transform you. Our lives are not meant to be static. We as humans do best and are at our happiest when we are always learning, moving forward, expanding our awareness, and seeking beyond the horizon.

We are like trees. If we are no longer growing, chances are we are dying. When you have accepted the loss of your mother and felt the transformational power of her continuing presence as part of your life, a triumphant sense can come over you. You can feel a deeper understanding, a new appreciation, a new sense of connection to your mother and all those around you, and indeed an inner knowing of the oneness and continuity of all life.

In this new seventh stage, which I call the stage of Triumph, you can feel a new sense of maturity, of confidence in your own direction whatever that may be, and of an inner and cosmic guidance which informs your daily decisions as well as your major ones. Whether it is your mother watching over you from afar or a more cosmic sense of the oneness of all, the sense of Triumph can be very real.

Though in the first year this sense of Triumph may feel a long way off, it is important to know that stories evolve and yours will too. Help is available through the compassionate camaraderie of others and through your own kindness to yourself. There is every reason for hope for easier days as you take the steps you need to take to help you to let go of your earthly mother and incorporate her lasting gifts.

With the help of the stories you are hearing here in *Mothers Losing Mothers*, I trust that you will gain new confidence in your own personal journey, in your own timing, in your own stages of mourning, now expanded to seven, and in your own strategies for continuing to grow and glow through it all. You can be an active participant in that grand process of creating a life and feel triumphant as your new life unfolds.

Keep in mind then the Seven T's which I have outlined here, and trust that you will be glad you gave yourself the time, energy, and love which you deserve as you experience the processes of mind, body, and spirit in healing from the loss of your mother:

- Tragedy
- Torment
- Transition
- Trial
- Tranquility
- Transformation
- Triumph

Trust your feelings as they flow from one to another. Your eventual sense of transformation and triumph over the trials and adversity we each must face on this unique human voyage can eventually become a beacon to others on similar paths.

The strength of a nation, especially of a republican nation, is in the intelligent and well-ordered homes of the people.
LYDIA H. SIGOURNEY

CHAPTER 10

SUSAN'S STORY: BLUE HYACINTHS

My mother passed away at 9:20 on July 29th, 2009. She was 84. It was evening, right after she had dinner with my brother Buzz. I wonder if most people demise in the evening.

It would have been still somewhat light there on the west coast of Florida at that time in July. It was about 30 days after the summer solstice, so the days were getting shorter. But the sun does set about half an hour later on the west side of Florida than it does here in Pennsylvania.

She did not go to New Hampshire that summer. Her fear of falling was so extreme by then that she felt a huge sense of relief when Dad went alone to their beloved spot on Squam Lake and she stayed in Florida. She got great solace knowing Dad was where he wanted to be.

Thus over the summer we were all taking turns visiting Mom down in Florida, and the boys, my brothers, were going up to see Dad in New Hampshire. I was here in Pennsylvania on July 29th with plans to go down and visit on the 30th. But she didn't wait for me.

My first reaction was "How could you, Mom? You knew I was coming!" And usually older people hold on, waiting to see somebody. Buzz had prepared me that I would be rather shocked at Mom's appearance. So maybe it was that, maybe she didn't want me to see her that way, although Mom was not vain at all.

When she had dinner with Buzz that evening, they had gone to the dining room at her retirement facility, which means Mom puts on nicer clothes and undoubtedly a necklace and earrings and stuff.

She would always make an effort to look nice to go down and dine. Even on the last night.

Since I was at the home site of the family burial plot here in Pennsylvania, I made all the arrangements for church, for funeral director, and for getting the box of her ashes sent from Florida to up here.

The thought of cremation shocked Dad. But interstate transportation of a whole body is logistically very difficult. I believe there are all kinds of special certifications to do that. FedEx and UPS will not transport ashes. The ash box had to come by U.S. Mail.

I didn't want it sent to my house, and our church really didn't want it. I now know for future reference, it's from funeral home to funeral home. But it took many, many phone calls to establish that.

With all those arrangements, Mom's memorial service wasn't until August 11th. It was a nice length of time to get all in order. Once the plan was established, my wonderful Uncle Tom, Mom's brother, Mom's only relative, secured the Merion Cricket Club for us for the reception. This was instead of the Gulf Mills Golf Club, which Dad adored, but Dad thought it would be too festive.

And I said, "Okay, Dad." And it was a searingly hot, sunny August day for the service. Since the Church of the Redeemer was being renovated, the main church was closed, and all services were being held in the tiny little Parish House Assembly Room. We thought that was too small.

Churches work together around here. If a church is sidelined, another church will come to its aid. Men tend to follow the wife's religion. Uncle Tom had been raised Episcopalian like Mom, but he married a Presbyterian. So we chose Bryn Mawr Presbyterian, which is huge. It holds 800. I was thinking, "Oh my God, we're going to be echoing and rattling around in that huge church!"

Well, more than 300 people came.

They cut short their vacation for Dad, to support Dad. We had a wonderful, wonderful lady minister. Thank goodness Dad was all right with that. You didn't know what would start him being upset again, maybe, so I made all those arrangements. It turned out that her father went to Yale like Dad and she talked in the most wonderful cadence. She was perfect for it.

We learned from her that one could change words of a reading: If you took a reading from Ecclesiastes, for example, you could remove a word. Dad didn't want the word "war" in something that we had chosen. I'm standing there being rigid, saying, "Dad, I'm sure you can't change words of the Bible." But she said it was all right to remove it. She said people can say anything you want.

Dad wanted special hard paper for the program. I went to Staples twice to get him the right kind of paper. So it was all about pleasing Dad in the weirdest ways in all that time. I had to make sure I had wheat germ in the house, because that's what he likes on his cereal at breakfast. And blueberries or strawberries or raspberries – good for the antioxidants. He preferred blueberries, only one percent milk, and all this. I have it down pretty much to a science about what Dad likes. And so there was that too.

So the service went well. I did all the flowers, and that was very cathartic. It was just a very inspiring turnout. And more came to the service than came to the reception, where they could have at least gotten some libation or something.

We looked at the book later. This is why the book that people sign at the service is so important. Since so many came just to the service, if I encountered any of them later, I could still thank them for coming. Otherwise, if they weren't at the reception, I wouldn't have known that they were there.

Dad is 86. He is in excellent health. In his golf game he shoots less than his age. He plays golf three or four times a week. This is why Mom and Dad went to The Moorings in Florida for the winter rather than Beaumont or Waverly around here – because you can't really golf around here in winter and golf was Dad's passion. It kept him healthy. And the networking was unbelievable. The heads of industry and banks all played, back when banking was a "gentleman's" profession. It's just mind-boggling whom Dad has met on the senior golf tour. It's been very impressive – our eyes opened rather wide when Dad said he played with so-and-so, and so-and-so who used to be head of RJR Nabisco or something. So Dad is fine, mentally and physically there.

Dad is host of the World War II Marine Corps Flyers' luncheon every year down in Florida. Attendance diminishes every year but there is great esprit de corps.

As children of World War II veterans, our generation, I think, has in general a stronger work ethic than our children's generation. We are willing to be of service, whereas our children will work more for money and a certain lifestyle. A fierce patriotism drove them to enlist, work, or volunteer for the war effort. We baby boomers inherited their sense of duty.

As an American Civilization major, I gave a talk on that subject at a Garden Club of America Convention. I had to answer the question, "Why did you say yes to being president?" I cited that history. I said our fathers were in the service; we believe in service. The big lament is that it's so hard to have younger members say yes anymore to doing anything on any club projects.

I think my three brothers have said that I can sound like our mother Halsey, not in timber or anything, but the words I say. But I don't feel more powerful or empowered since her death. Maybe it's a little different for me, because I'm the only girl and the oldest. So I always had it.

At this stage now – I think it started around Christmas time – we can fondly recall Mom, and relate about situations, and laugh and just freely say, at any time, "Now Mom would have done this," or "Do you remember this and this?" It's so nice to be on this plateau now, rather than be in fear of dredging up sadness, the way it was when the loss was still so raw.

For Christmas, youngest brother Tom set up an itinerary for Dad to get him out of Florida, so he wouldn't wake up on Christmas morning alone. I was horrified at that thought. So Dad flew to Seattle via Colorado, and then back here and saw all four of his children. The travel was not easy or pleasant, but David got him flying first class all the way. He had good visits with all of us and then returned home in time for New Year's Eve, for which he had had a date for months. Women can sense a widower miles away.

He was happy to return to Florida. So that was nice, rather than having him enduring the family holidays without anybody there. It certainly was easier to have one person move all around than all four of us descend on him, for which there was no room in the apartment in Florida anyhow.

I was pleased that Dad was up to the travel. I would have dressed him better, but then again .... He wore a red and green plaid blazer that probably harkened back to 1950, because it was

Christmas time. And I just kind of winced when he walked in the door, but that's all right.

So many things I will just see that happen every day, and I will go, "Mom would like that," like nature programs on television or history programs.

When packing for a trip I note so many things Mom has given me or we bought together. It's kind of like packing Mom.

All of her good clothes, of course, are still in this house, because I'm waiting for the Community Clothes Charity event in October, where they document every item, tag it, and give it a number, so that when it is sold, it is carefully documented who gave it. They will then send a professional accountant letter with the sum for the donation, which I can give to Dad. And I will have to record every single item and I'll have it on a hanger before I take it to the location in Strafford. These clothes are all too big for me, which is hard to believe because Mom was quite small the last time I saw her. I feel this project is kind of a way to honor Mom for Dad. So all these clothes are sitting down there waiting.

I removed all the clothes in Florida. I even took her lipsticks to a school dramatic department. Mom had 25 of the same color lipsticks. I found them in all her evening purses. I emptied all the evening purses into one drawer. There were so many from their trips abroad. When I emptied them, I would find money, I would find place cards, and I would find Kleenex and a lipstick.

Some of the bags from her trips to Italy with her mom were of beautiful Moroccan leather, but they have the short strap, so I can't put it over my shoulder. I'm giving those to the Community Clothes Charity also. And they will put a price tag of probably $200 or something on it. They don't use thrift prices for really good things.

Then there were the accumulated bandages among her things. There was so much in stock never used, never opened, and I couldn't give them back to the facility at The Moorings, where she was staying, so I took them to a clinic in Naples, Florida. A friend of Mom's drove me all around to drop all these things off.

That was nice. I hated throwing things away. So we found a place for everything.

Dad wanted to keep one shirt because it still smelled like Mom. He teared up when he told me that. About every fifth phone call with me he'll mention that. It would be interesting to see if he brings it up to New Hampshire with him. It's in his top drawer in Florida.

Dad and my brother Tom cleared out all the New Hampshire stuff in August and brought it down before the service. A lot of it was L.L. Bean style, more for the New England woods. I gave that to the church thrift shop. And anything that was really nice and was really special to Dad, I divvied between me and my three sisters-in-law.

I haven't tackled the silver. Dad still lives down there in Florida so he can use it. I haven't tackled the silver or all the pictures on Mom's bedroom bureau.

I wanted these to stay at that house. I don't want them in this house. Mostly they are duplicates. In those young-children days, we'd get a 5x7 of the children and give one to Mom and Dad for Christmas, as all three brothers did with their children. So there tend to be duplicates.

Now, I can delay dealing with all the pictures, because I think Dad wants the bureau to stay like she had it. He remembers to water the plants. There aren't as many as back in the day, but I tell him it's good for him to have a plant in the house, and so he will think of that.

I have no idea what New Hampshire is going to be like. I did not go up there last August after Mom died. If I had gone up there and eventually all three brothers came up as usual, I would have become Mom. I would have become the one to market, to cook, and to do laundry. There would have been absolutely no vacation for me.

Incredibly selfish of me, I suppose. How did the rotation between the three brothers and wives go? Not well organized. Apparently each person would do dinner and go out and buy a new set of supplies, so when it was time for Dad to close the house and come south, there were ten mustards, five of something else. There were so many duplications because no one had done a careful inventory before doing their assigned meal. I think it was very stressful for all.

People nicely tell me I was wise. I could be serene in the garden here and think of Mom as I dug and dug and dug. I had it easier. And then all of them would call me and tell me how difficult it was, but they could cite grief and missing me without actually saying there was no mom there to do all the drudge work, which of course would have been me.

Before, I tended to be up there for five weeks, so that Mom and I could go to antique shows, decoupage together, garden, and get ready for the next batch of visitors coming. As a team, it was fun. And Mom would make dinner and I could be down on the dock. So I could still be a child. I wasn't going to go up there now and not be allowed to be a child. I would have become wife and mother to everybody.

That decision was hard. I think it was slightly mean to Dad for me not to go, but then, of course, he would gripe that, "Well, your mother used to make it this way. Your mother used to do it this way." So I protected myself also by not having to hear that.

Thinking about Mom's experience of mothering and my own, Mom flew in after the birth of each of my children and would take some night duty to help me out. They weren't living here; they were traveling a lot because Dad was on the Visa board and Visa always met in exotic places. But always as the only daughter, thank goodness, she would come and just help with all the chores.

So when my daughter Amanda had Halsey, named after Mom and two weeks old yesterday, I said, "Amanda, how often do you want me there?" I asked her rather than just forcing myself on her at her house. So I find myself copying Mom in trying to be there for her. That is very good.

Career-wise, as a mother, when I was working I had only the two children. By the time my third child was born, I had stopped work. Mom thought my working was fine, though she did not work except as a volunteer when we were children. Working at Lilly Pulitzer kept me sane: childcare took up most of my salary. Mom was accepting of my work, and she loved Lilly. When volunteer things overlapped and I would get stressed, she would ask, "Why do you volunteer so much?"

When you work from 9 to 5, you have one job and then there's your family life. Volunteer things can be all over the calendar or hit on the same date, or a commitment for A overlaps with B, which you don't allow to happen with just one job. So that is when she counseled about doing too much.

We did not spend money on travel, because I hate to travel, yet Mom would insist we take anniversary trips. So she came and took care of the children, and we went to Bermuda, to Hawaii, and to Switzerland. She would do school, do lunches, and do absolutely everything.

Two years ago we went to England, Mom was overjoyed; she gave me her *Lady's Book to London* and told me where we should go, which we followed practically to the letter. Mom loved to travel, whereas I did not. But I was always glad we did go.

That was a wonderful part of her. If part of being a mother is telling grown-up children what to do, it is true that when we followed her travel command, it was always very rewarding. It wasn't the time factor or the monetary factor of traveling. It was just me and my fear of getting lost. So it was very nice that she did that, and with Charlie I always felt very secure, so I enjoyed it.

Mom really knew her antiques as did her mother. I have a strong sense of my own interior design. I wanted Mom to display things or to have rooms arranged in such and such a way. It would really bother me when things weren't neat. That wasn't really a source of friction, but there we were really apart – she wanted comfy and cozy, whereas I wanted to look like *House Beautiful*.

During the war, Mom and her brother grew up with a couple, Mary and Leroy. They were the cook, chauffeur, and handyman. So it's not as if they were bereft during the war and Mom would be overcompensating with stuff. It just wasn't neat. And that was compounded by the fact that Dad rarely threw anything away, so golf magazines going back four years would just drive me nuts. I have a very low threshold for disarray, whereas Mom could tolerate a much higher one.

I remember I would get upset with Mom when she was older and we would go shopping together – mostly in Florida. In Naples, the small clothing stores were very chic. Mom rarely bought designer clothing even though their precision cut was slimming and snappy.

She would say, "No Susan, I want to be comfortable." So, it was jackets with big necks and elastic waist bands and Aerosole brand shoes.

Mom would say simply, "That appealed to me." So all these clothes that appealed to Mom are hanging up in Amanda's closet or hanging downstairs. And it's a sea of blue and green, or black, whereas I'm so pink.

The only time I really tear up is when I go to visit Mom's new gravestone and tell her about my granddaughter Halsey and my children.

I tell Dad I go and visit and I think that pleases him. Dad certainly will visit when he comes up from Florida. He's probably going to want me to plant something on her. I think I'm going to plant some blue hyacinths. I love flowers. Mom enjoyed gardening and appreciated flowers, but she wasn't as into it as I am. She had lots of house plants. In Florida there wasn't a garden, but in New Hampshire there was always a garden.

With low humidity in New Hampshire, certain plants could always weather the summer, whereas here in Pennsylvania they wither. I would buy late blooming perennials, preferably in blue, and plant, prune, and weed. With no deer there, all flourished.

In golf tournaments, you tend to get some big gift, as well you should, because it costs you about $500 to enter, which covers your food, your greens fees, and everything else. Then you're invariably given something specifically from that golf club, and oftentimes it's a very large framed print of hole number four or the great waterhole out off of the ninth tee. Mom would always dutifully make room for Dad to hang that picture. Now, some of them did get hung behind doors.

Goodbyes were especially long with my family. The last time I saw Mom was in March, a few months before she died. Then, things were on the up and up. So there was no foreboding. And at that time, all systems were go for spending her summer in New Hampshire. That time with her was reassuring and healthy. That helped all of us.

After the car accident in October 2008, Mom's reading declined, and she just adored reading. She still did play bridge. I always felt as though Mom's pill regimen made her fuzzy. Dad would ask the doctor again and again for editing of the pill list. One of us children was visiting Dad every single month since the accident. So in November, December, and January, we were all taking turns. When Amanda and I came down in January of 2009, we spent one whole day returning books and decks of cards which visitors had brought. They had all been on the dining room table. It was just overwhelming. There were over 300 get-well cards, which I then put in order by date, while combining people, because some people would send one every week, "Thinking of you," "Glad to hear you're getting better," and so on.

I had them all organized, and then Mom said she didn't want to keep any of them. That made sense. Keeping cards makes you look back. Letters are another thing, but I have heard this about keeping cards, like all the Mother's Day cards that my children give me. I kept them, because it was evidence of changing handwriting and growing up, but I have tossed them. I thought it was very healthy.

I do believe Dad has kept every single letter of condolence he received, which I put in a nice festive, handled bag. I can organize stuff for Dad but I can't throw it away. He abides with that, knowing that it's just me and my super organization.

One helpful thought which I heard recently at a memorial service was that we gather together – come here today, not to mourn the death of so-and-so but to celebrate their life. I had never heard that before. That idea consoles.

Now, for some reason when I hear the word celebration, I think you should have someone sing. I find a soloist rather sad, whereas the Orpheus Club chorus sings magnificently for a deceased club member.

I save programs now from funerals, because there's always some special thing that I really admire: like a child's drawing for a great-grandmother or an extensive family tree.

Only with respect to Mom do I envision – I don't know if it came from a book or a movie or what – that she is up there with her parents and all of her departed friends and having a wonderful time and eating whatever she wants. She loved chocolate and there she won't get fat! But she's probably wearing the same blue and green clothes.

I see her just as the lovely smiling mom that we have pictures of. My brothers were adamant about framing some pictures to have at the reception. They copied and downloaded shiny-sheeted prints of pictures they had of Mom and brought the prints with them when they flew in to town for the reception. When they got here, they went throughout my house and took all the frames they needed for the pictures. At least it was their idea, and it really pleased Dad.

As for advice for other women going through this experience, well, you sure do remember the good times. If you remember the battles with your mom over some teenage lack of liberty or anything, I think you can laugh at it now. I had a wonderful relationship with Mom all through married life. Remember that the best parts of her made you what you are.

How often will you be mistaken for your mom? Often. You will smile, identify yourself, and be grateful. Mom and the blue hyacinths will live on.

Trouble is a part of your life, and if you don't share it, you don't give the person who loves you enough chance to love you enough.
DINAH SHORE

CHAPTER 11

THINGS YOU SHOULD AVOID

In this chapter you will find out all the awful things you will avoid by taking good care of yourself through this period around the loss of your mother. Lots of natural processes take time and energy. This one is no exception. It might seem easier to just take a sleeping pill when the sorrow, doubts, and burdens gang up on you. Or just take an anti-depressant when your painful emotions get stuffed to the back of your mind and make it harder to do your work or hard for anything to make you smile. Or get a prescription for anxiety when your hands shake making one more inquiry about your mother's bank accounts or insurance policies. Or succumb to guilt because you didn't get to say what you wanted to your mother, or because you didn't fight hard enough with the doctor or with your sibling about the course of care. Or lose faith in yourself because you can't live up to what you think your mother expected of you or who you think she was.

But what I have learned is that self-destructive behaviors don't solve problems. They only appear to hide them for a while. What has worked for me and many others is to handle what you have to do by imagining what your mother would have wanted you to do, deep down in her most essential spiritual self. And that is, of course, to be the best you you can be: the best mother, the best lover, the best friend, the best citizen, the best person you know how to be. And that's that.

Guilt, waning self-esteem, self-blame, or disempowerment are surely not what she would have in mind for you. She would want you to take the time and energy to integrate what good she brought to your life into your life now, to empower you to be who you want to be in all your glory, as a spiritual being yourself.

So don't hide from the task of letting go of your mother. Just as we as children naturally and unconsciously integrated the precognitive messages we got from our mothers into our very assumptions about life, it is now our job to follow a similar path, this time consciously, cognitively, but also again naturally, to integrate our mothers into our lives, to empower ourselves to be worthy of their mother love.

All the world's religious and spiritual traditions, as well as our own survival instincts and evolutionary imperatives, call on us to honor our mothers. And this is the way we can do it now.

It is a difficult process, with lots of pain, but the alternative is not feeling at all or dragging ourselves through a painful life looking for solutions in all the wrong places. Instead, as we move through the seven T stages, from tragedy to triumph, we can find true serenity, health, and happiness.

Best not to ignore the impact

There are serious consequences to trying to ignore, deny, or suppress your pain. You can avoid these consequences by being a compassionate observer of your own process, trusting that it will get better. There are a number of ways we can try to ignore our pain but they all have consequences and not good ones. We can try to keep ourselves so busy that we can't think of our pain, we can adopt certain mind-altering habits which appear to hide our pain, or we can medicate ourselves with pain meds. None of these bring us out of the tunnel in good shape. Let's take a look at them.

Many mothers dive into their work, their job, or their home responsibilities and declare themselves too busy to really address the issues they know are in their minds when their mother has passed. For example, they may just purchase this book and then let it sit on the shelf. That's okay. I want you to trust your own timing. I have done that with many a book. I bought it because I knew I would benefit, but I didn't get around to it until months or even years later. But I have always been glad I bought the book. I have learned to trust my own timing, because the books I do read appear always to be at exactly the time I can benefit most. This way I am ready to apply their good advice to my life right away and I maximize my benefits.

While putting off reading a book may do no harm, putting off dealing with your pain for too long can lead to long term damage which can manifest in depression, lethargy, loss of motivation, alienation, loss of romantic interest, failing health, and other ailments for which you may not later even know the cause, as I'll describe in a moment.

Dangerous distractions

What about smoking, drinking, over-eating, poor eating, or drugging? These can be non-medical ways of self-medicating our pain. Humans discovered many centuries ago ways to manipulate natural substances to create mood-altering effects. Whether it's alcohol from fermented grains or fruits, caffeine-like substances from coffee, tea, cola, or chocolate, nicotine from tobacco leaves, marijuana from hemp, sugar from cane, or some other natural brain teaser, you can always hide from your feelings with these. They have become acceptable social lubricants in various cultures and in moderation can do little harm. But taken too often, their toxic effects eventually far outweigh their benefits.

When you use these concentrated substances too often, shifts happen in your biological metabolism which lead to addiction and serious health and behavioral consequences. Whether you like it or not, your brain then calls out for more, and no one knows how much is too much for any individual until after their line has been crossed.

But even without going that far, you face the danger of hiding your feelings with these mind-benders, so that you get stuck in your forward progress and also you may risk the danger of bringing on health problems which themselves may hide your pain, such as loading up on sweet confections which can lead to indigestion, diabetes, and obesity, adding insult to injury. Meanwhile, these mind-altering substances can exaggerate as well as hide feelings, so moods can hit new highs and lows.

Now unfortunately we have found new ways of manipulating and concentrating mind-altering agents and have even invented new ones in the lab. Obviously these agents are severely damaging even in small quantities by definition, being totally alien to the body and therefore toxins. Don't hide your pain with these.

If we add to the use of mind-altering substances other distractions taken to excess, like gambling, video-gaming, or sexual obsession, we see other self-sabotaging behaviors which can easily be adopted or exaggerated by the trauma of loss. The experience of Alcoholics Anonymous and the many other 12-Step Self-Help Groups it has led to over the past 60 years have shown that these self-destructive habits are self-reinforcing based on emotional pain. When folks are hungry, angry, lonely, or tired, they find these stimulants or depressants to help them hide from the real cause of their troubles. Serious personal loss, here the loss of your mother, can be a launch-pad in disguise for addictive, self-destructive behaviors.

The long recognized antidote is self-awareness and positive, frequent sharing with others who know what you are going through because of their own experience.

Unrecognized inner causes

But now imagine just how many mothers may have become depressed or anxious after their mothers' demise, or during a prolonged parent-care period, without realizing what caused their bad feelings, because the society won't acknowledge how profound a loss she has suffered. Many emotions during this time may be seen as personality changes requiring medical attention, as if you had become suddenly a depressed, angry, difficult, or unmotivated person. If you or those around you don't allow you the time and space you need to feel and appreciate the full impact of losing your mother, then it is easy to conclude that something is wrong with you. You may come to that conclusion yourself.

This is when our society comes up with medicinal drug solutions. Because of all the mood-altering medications developed in recent decades, your doctor can offer you drugs for your depression, for your anger, for your irritability, for your lack of motivation, or even for your loss of libido. My grandmother's husband was killed in a boating accident when my father was just five years old, and she was never allowed to recover. She was on medications until the day she died, over 35 years later. I know the impact on my father was profound, though he never spoke of it.

These medications may help get you through a difficult period, but they will not substitute for the essential process of coming to grips with the pain of loss. They can prevent you from moving on through the process of recovery from the loss. And they can also lead to a life of changed personality as well as various unwanted side-effects, since they are all chemicals which are not normal to the body and will inevitably have toxic effects in the long run.

How many people can a mother's pain affect? Are her children confused by it, because they think her change of mood or impatient or tearful outbursts are because of them? Is her husband frustrated because she can't quite handle her usual responsibilities, or loses romantic interest, or seems to be acting suddenly "just like your mother"? Is she less effective on the job, not communicating as well, falling behind, not her usual cheerful, conscientious self?

Millions of wonderful women are being tormented in silence by the failure of society as a whole and in many cases also friends, family, and helping professionals to recognize, honor, accommodate, and give vent and ceremony to this important passage in a daughter-mother's life. And recall that there are 10 to 20 million of us.

The dangers of overmedication

I want to consider briefly here how so many women today may be getting caught by the epidemic of mind-altering medications without even knowing it. After experiencing for my self the changes, mostly temporary, wrought by my mother's death in my own feelings, I came to wonder, how many medications are issued to mothers who know they want to and must continue on with their responsibilities as mothers and wives and also must take on the settling of their mother's affairs and the mourning process as well, doing the latter almost entirely on their own, in silence? Psychiatrist Robert E. Kay, MD, recently told me that even if a professional recognizes that a patient is suffering from prolonged grief, grief itself is now being viewed as a disease for which medication can be prescribed. He was very concerned about this trend.

Imagine how many over-the-counter and prescription medications for sleeplessness, anxiety, depression, fatigue, listlessness, and energy boosts may be purchased by mothers who have lost their mothers and are feeling overwhelmed, misunderstood, and alone. What doctor has time to find out why she is feeling this way?

In his book *Medication Madness: A Psychiatrist Exposes the Dangers of Mood-Altering Medications*, Dr. Peter R. Breggin attacks the epidemic of 200 million psychiatric drug prescriptions written annually and exposes how so many of them are inappropriate and dangerous. He describes the dangers of these medications and gives real life stories of their destructive effects. He also explains how so often there is a real cause for the patient's distress which could have been addressed, but doctors and their patients are "spellbound" by the idea that the drugs will do the work.

Prescriptions for depression and anxiety are topping the charts in numbers of prescriptions and show no signs of slowing down. Recently pharmaceutical companies have introduced new lines of drugs with psychotropic properties to respond to these symptoms. And hurried, harried doctors are willing to prescribe whatever the pharmaceutical companies suggest for these conditions. No one is asking these patients if they have had a loss or trauma in the last year or two.

Yet they may be drowning the pain of their loss and ultimately suffering physical harm as a result of drugs they don't really need. In a recent article in the *AARP Bulletin*,[11] Donald W.

Light, author of *The Risks of Prescription Drugs*, pointed out that drowsiness, sleeplessness, muscle aches, dizziness, nausea, depression, trouble with balance, slower reaction times, gastric problems, and muscle pain can be side effects of commonly prescribed drugs which can interfere with daily activities and mood.

In the same AARP article, Gordon Schiff, M.D., internist on the Harvard Medical School Faculty and associate director of the Brigham Center for Patient Safety Research and Practice, is quoted as saying that drugs which treat the side effects of other drugs end up building a "house of cards" which can tumble down to the patient's detriment. He recommends that doctors "think beyond drugs" and discuss lifestyle changes with patients.

According to the article, 4.5 million visits a year to doctors' offices or emergency rooms are due to serious drug reactions. According to Michael Steinman, M.D., associate professor at UC San Francisco, drug tests for safety are typically performed using subjects who are young and healthy. Before a drug is introduced or even for 7 to 10 years later, it is seldom known, according to the experts, how it will affect older people and especially those older people who are already taking other medications.

Baby boomers at risk

Between the years 2000 and 2008, deaths caused by accidental overdoses of prescription drugs had tripled among people aged 50 to 69, according to *a Los Angeles Times* analysis of data obtained from the Centers for Disease Control and Prevention. This is the age group we are concerned about here. Our mothers gave birth to the baby boom and are now leaving us. In 2012, baby boom mothers are 48 to 66.

Is relying on chemicals to treat our feelings one of the not-so-great trends we baby boomers are responsible for? Mick Jagger sang about "mother's little helpers" when we were teenagers. And our generation was famous for trying to alter our moods and

---

[11] Patricia Barry, "The Side Effects of Side Effects," *AARP Bulletin,* September 2011, http://pubs.aarp.org/aarpbulletin/201109_DC?folio=14#article_id=104698.

consciousness with chemicals. Now this trend comes back to haunt our middle years.

Unfortunately, the emotional denial of the pain of losing a loved one and the drive to sell more and more patented drugs is a powerful combination which puts folks who are in pain at additional risk.

I hope this book will allow you and other women in pain to seek real support and help in moving through this most unsettling passage and in finding new firm ground to stand on which builds on the legacy your mother has left for you and gives birth to a welcome future of fulfillment and happiness.

If you try to hide from emotional pain by stuffing it, your body still will know. In addition to the mental effects which can occur if the pain of loss is denied, left unrecognized, or medicated away, unresolved hurt can create direct physical effects too, effects on your health and even on that of your family.

Your body knows

A recent study demonstrated that loss of a loved one can literally break your heart. Published in the journal *Circulation*, the study examined people who had suffered heart attacks to find out if they had recently suffered the loss of a "significant person" in their lives. Lead author Elizabeth Mostofsky and her team compared these results with any losses in the previous six months or year of the patients' lives. They found that, "Losing someone raises the risk of having a heart attack the next day by 21-fold, and the risk of a heart attack in the following week by six times. The apparently broken hearts showed signs of mending after about a month, when risk of heart attacks started to decline."[12]

American women are raised not to complain, particularly baby boomer women, who were reminded, rightly though perhaps too often, that we had more advantages than any generation in

------

[12] Alice Park, "How Grief Can Break Your Heart," *Time Healthland,* http://healthland.time.com/2012/01/10/how-grief-can-break-your-heart/ (10 January 2012).

history. Also, we are proud of being independent and self-sufficient and often hate to admit we need help.

Meanwhile, this misguided thinking is reinforced when we let it be known that we are in emotional pain and we are told to get over it, to move on, to deal with it, to stop bothering others about it, to take a pill.

So what do we do? We can stuff our feelings, forget why we hurt, and suddenly develop a bad back, a sore shoulder, a stiff neck, headaches, frequent colds, allergies, digestive problems, a twisted ankle, or a bad knee. We can usually find some recent activity to attribute the problem to, but it is often also an activity we do often enough that we are surprised it could lead to this. Of course, repetitive activity can lead to stress or soreness, but is it true in every case?

According to Dr. John E. Sarno, as described in his most recent book *The Divided Mind: The Epidemic of MindBody Disorders,*[13] chronic pain is often present not from any particular physical cause but from a psychological or emotional cause. He and his colleagues have dealt with thousands of cases where when one physical cause is investigated and treated, another kind of pain in a different part of the body emerges in short order.

He finds that if he helps these patients acknowledge their previous emotional wounds or even simply helps them to appreciate that their pain may be a resting place for long forgotten emotional stresses, then the localized pain will go away without any further recurrences elsewhere. I have no doubt that the loss of one's mother, especially coupled with a mother's deep appreciation for what it means to be a mother and the realization that you are next in line to go, could be such a cause of chronic physical pain.

Pain prescriptions have been among the fastest growing in the medication marketplace in the last few years. And it is no accident that medical prescriptions are up more than 40% since pharmaceutical advertising was permitted on TV. Other countries do

---

[13] John E. Sarno, MD, *The Divided Mind: The Epidemic of MindBody Disorders* (New York: HarperCollins, 2006).

not permit direct-to-consumer advertising of prescription drugs. Coupled with the mandatory coverage of prescriptions by Medicare, it is just so easy for people to believe that a pill which they don't even have to pay much for will solve their chronic pain. The colorful graphics on the screen showing baby boomers rubbing their backs, unable to bend their knees, afraid to go outside for fear of pollen, or wincing at churning in their stomachs, can too easily convince us that the advertised drug will do the trick.

Listen with a healthy skepticism

In a *New England Journal of Medicine* article titled, "A Decade of Direct-to-Consumer Advertising of Prescription Drugs,"[14] the authors began with this observation: "Evidence suggests that direct-to-consumer advertising of prescription drugs increases pharmaceutical sales and both helps to avert underuse of medicines and leads to potential overuse. Concern about such advertising has increased recently owing to the withdrawal from the market of heavily advertised drugs found to carry serious risks. Moreover, the Food and Drug Administration (FDA) has been criticized for its weak enforcement of laws regulating such advertising."

The authors pointed out that just between 2002 and 2004 expenditures on drug advertising increased from 2.9 billion dollars to 4.2 billion dollars, while the FDA only added one person to the three responsible for examining and approving TV drug ads. Meanwhile, the backlog in the reviewing process has become so serious that many letters of disapproval go out only after the drug ad campaign has already finished and the population has already been exposed.

The authors also noted a concern that the advertising of new drugs immediately after their introduction appeared to increase their sales while the evidence of safety in the field was not yet optimal. Hence, the recall of so many new drugs. The most popular

---

[14] Julie M. Donohue, Ph.D., Marisa Cevasco, B.A., and Meredith B. Rosenthal, Ph.D., "A Decade of Direct-to-Consumer Advertising of Prescription Drugs," *N Engl J Med* 2007; 357:673-681, August 16, 2007.

prescription pain drug today is Vicodin. Along with the other most popular pain drugs, it is the most common drug implicated in deaths by overdose. These drugs are particularly dangerous combined with other drugs or alcohol. How many busy women in midlife are reaching for a prescription instead of turning to a friend or relative who can comfort her in her pain?

How many of these drugs to help us cope with various physical pains are causing negative effects that are wholly unnecessary because the root cause is not physical? It is well known that stress causes all kinds of physical changes in our bodies, and the death of a mother is a major stress, especially for a busy woman who is not only a mother herself but probably also has a job and has perhaps spent a couple of years caring for her ailing mother.

So unfortunately the trend in dealing with the loss of a loved one is, like in so many other areas of our lives, to look for a quick fix, often a chemical fix. But this can lead to relationship problems, growing physical problems, side effects from the drugs, and deep unhappiness, with little understanding of the underlying cause.

With *Mothers Losing Mothers*, my hope is that you will appreciate the natural process of mourning and recovery that follows on the death of your mother and will be able to stop short of resorting to poor substitutions for the very human endeavor of welcoming the initial pain, the responsibilities, and the eventual gratification of moving on from one generation to another, and from tragedy to triumph.

I looked on child rearing not only as a work of love and duty but as a profession that was fully as interesting and challenging as any honorable profession in the world and one that demanded the best I could bring to it.
ROSE KENNEDY

CHAPTER 12

PAM'S STORY: CANDY STRIPES

My mother died one day short of her 89th birthday, on February 6th, 2009. She was born in 1920. My father had died on my birthday two years previous to that.

My parents were divorced when I was four and they really didn't have any contact with each other. I didn't have much contact with my father when I was growing up, but as I became an adult we established a pretty close relationship, and I was actually with him when he passed away. With my mother, I wanted to be with her, but my family and I had gone out to eat. The hospice nurse had come to enroll her in hospice and it was late Friday night. My niece and nephew were there from New York and we hadn't had anything to eat for a number of hours, so we stepped out to get a meal and she passed away then.

I would have liked to have been with her, but I feel like I was with her a lot in the days before, and I think she knew that I was with her in spirit. What my pastor said, which I thought was a little bit comforting and maybe possible, was that maybe she just decided she was ready and didn't want to burden me with being there. I don't know.

With my dad, I knew he was dying. He lived in Connecticut and my stepmom called me and said, "You should come if you want to be here." So I got in my car and drove up and he died within a half hour, with she and I present. So maybe there is something to the idea that they decide when they want to go and who they want to have with them.

Mom's death certificate listed dementia, but really she had a number of issues. She had really bad arthritis, which caused her great pain, mostly in her hip. She had always been active, so that was difficult for her. Her precipitating problem at the time of her death was that she had had a fall. She was simply getting up from the table in the dining room where she lived in the Waverly retirement community, and somehow she missed her walker and she fell. So they took her to the hospital.

Fortunately she did not break a hip, which of course is the great killer of the elderly, often precipitating their death. But when she was in the hospital, she seemed to develop some kind of bug – a very bad lung infection. She was in the hospital for a while. Then she started to go into renal failure. She was developing painful and severe muscle atrophy where her muscles became all tight – it was so painful to move her. And she really wanted to go.

I stayed overnight with her in the hospital and I heard her say very clearly – and she really wasn't talking much then – "God, take me home."

I was the person who was to make her decisions. With the kidney failure, a renal specialist came in and said, "Well, we can try giving her blood." They basically felt that that would be a way, possibly, to get her kidneys functioning again. But she had a living will which refused that. So I was in conflict about it. I figured it was a fairly benign kind of treatment for her, and it was before I heard her say what she said.

So I okayed the transfusion for her, and for the first couple days it didn't seem to be making much difference. She was on an oncology floor even though she did not have cancer, and finally one of the nurses that I really liked came to me and said, "Well, what are you going to do here? With her age and everything, are you gonna – what are you thinking?"

I was already thinking that with the muscle atrophy probably not going to get better and with the process of the therapy and everything, what she would have to endure would be terrible. By then I had heard her say that statement. So basically I asked them to put her on comfort care.

But then the doctor who put her on this treatment came in – he hadn't read her chart – and said, "Oh, she's improving." Oh boy. That was not helpful. You just wish people would really take the time to read the chart, but whatever. By that time, the decision had been made.

I felt like it was what she wanted, even though at that time in her life my mom had a wonderful relationship with a widower, and they were constant companions. And he is now 102 and still survived her. He's an incredible man. I had tried to include him, get him to see her as much as possible at the end. I tried to keep him kind of in the loop on things. I felt bad for him in a way when I made that decision, but I still felt like it was what my mom wanted, and her quality of life would probably be terrible. It's never easy, never smooth. Things happen unexpectedly. And I must say that even with her living will clearly in place and stating her wishes, the role of the health care agent who must ultimately make this important decision on behalf of her/his loved one is difficult, even in the best of circumstances. I would be less than honest if I did not say that I haven't second guessed that decision, gone over it in my mind many times, and wondered if I could have/should have let the situation play out in a different way. I can only hope and pray that this momentous decision was the best for Mom, and I am certain my intentions were the best.

They discontinued the treatment and put her on comfort care. She went back to Waverly and she actually died the day she returned to Waverly, which was unexpected. The hospice people thought she would possibly have another couple weeks, but she went really fast and maybe it's just, again, because she was ready. But her companion did have time with her that afternoon alone. I gave them time, and I spent some time, and my niece and nephew spent time, and everyone who was with her had that opportunity to say a fond goodbye. We tried to make it as good as we could.

Making those decisions is a big responsibility.

I have a brother, but at the time right before her death – he's a real free spirit kind of guy – he was hiking through the jungles of Mexico, and I couldn't even reach him till right before she passed. He did participate actively in her Memorial Service. As far as the decision making process, though, it's just as well that she appointed only me to handle her healthcare decisions.

My nephew and my niece were very helpful. And my husband was too, of course, but he was holding down the fort at home and taking care of the dog and all that. He would be supportive when I was home, but he was not physically with me. My nephew who is from New York City and my niece also from New York came down, and they were just wonderful.

My daughter would have been with me, except she lives in California. I did talk with her on the phone quite a lot. She has two children. My mother got to know them all. Although my mother's thinking was a little impaired the last couple years, when they would come east they would always visit her and she did absolutely enjoy her great-grandchildren.

Absorbing all the information and making all the decisions that needed to be made were both harder and easier because I am a nurse. Like everything, it was sort of a mixed deal. I feel like I was better able to understand what I was being told and understand the implications. At the same time, sometimes I may not have wanted to know some of the stuff. I guess it was better than not being a nurse. But you still have all the same feelings even if you have an understanding. It's not an intellectual thing as much as the feeling part you go through.

I think since my mom had dementia and, I guess, Alzheimer's, it was a whole long process for me of getting used to the changes as she aged. I think maybe that makes a little difference in terms of just dealing with the loss. My dad also had dementia. I don't know if this is just my thinking or if this is a reality, but I felt a little bit like with that particular disease, you are saying goodbye to the person you know in so many ways over time. Maybe it helps to ease that final goodbye more than if someone had a sudden kind of demise. There's no opportunity for that kind of slow process to happen. But then again, I have nothing to compare it with. It's only my assumption.

My mother started out independent when she moved in to the Waverly community. She was there for about 20 years. She moved through the system. When the time came that she needed assisted living, she moved into that section, and she was in assisted living for about two years before she advanced to skilled nursing, which was probably for her last year. The hard part for her was that she had a little dog that she loved and they let her keep the dog when she was in assisted living, but when she went into skilled nursing, obviously she could not have the dog anymore, and that was a terrible loss for her.

I took the dog, and I would bring the dog to visit Mom. Frankly, the dog was a bit of a pain. She never really learned house-training properly. My mother had gotten her as a rescue dog. I don't know what had happened to this poor little thing before, but she really was difficult. So that was an extra strain for me. The dog actually died about a month before Mom did. That was weird. The dog had sort of a seizure. They thought maybe she had a brain tumor. Maybe that was part of my mom's process. I don't know. She was so close to her dog. Even though my mom did not remember some things, she always remembered Toto.

Toto was sort of a mutt – a Pomeranian/Papillon, we figured. It was a teeny weeny little thing. I do believe dogs can be therapeutic for people. We've always had dogs. It's just the closeness with them, it's so relaxing.

As far as being the senior woman now in my family, I haven't really given that much thought. I don't think I even consciously had given it any consideration whatsoever when someone mentioned, "You're now the matriarch of your family," or whatever. I don't know that it's any different in that way.

But I do think about what it all means in terms of my own aging process. I think I was already thinking about that, just because my husband Ray was having some serious health issues. I think this whole process does encourage one to think about what time is left and the value of really making the most of every day.

I retired in January of 2010, almost a year after my mother's death.

Obviously I was planning to retire at some point. I hadn't really put a time on it, but Ray had retired the year before. So I was probably more pulled by the fact that he was at home and I wasn't, and that I was keeping us both from being able to do some things. We have a place down on the Chesapeake Bay, and we like to spend a lot of time there, but I was like a noose around his neck with my work obligations, besides the fact that we had this thought that we wanted to travel out to where our daughter is, get a trailer, and do more trips.

I'm sure that my mother's death played into my retirement decision in a subtle way. Frankly, we're able to do more in our retirement through just the generosity of her estate, which I hadn't given any thought to ahead of time. It has been a blessing to us. It allowed us to do some of the things that we probably couldn't have done otherwise. So her death did have an effect indirectly in that way.

I have little things that bring back memories of my mother, and they are pretty unpredictable. There's not one time of day, or one particular thing that does it for me, but suddenly I'll find myself saying, "Aah." It's like a jab or something.

I think to myself, "Oh, Mom, I could share this with you."

My daughter was close to my mom, but since she lives in California, she was very in touch by phone. She was actually ready to jump on a plane when my mom passed. She was going to try to get back to be with her, but she could not get there in time. We ended up having a memorial service about a month later, and Jen and the kids were there for that. But I know she was spiritually with us at the end, because they were close.

My husband still has his mom and we take care of her about every third weekend. His mom still is at home and lives with his sister, who works full-time, and we have caregivers come in when my sister-in-law is at work, for which we share the expense. We also get some help from the state. And then she comes and stays with us every third weekend, so his sister Beth Ann can have some down time.

His mom is a sweet woman. She also has some dementia. Other than that, she still seems to get around pretty much. Like so many people, she doesn't realize that some of the things she thinks she can do can be risky for her. She doesn't have the caution part left anymore in herself. So you have to keep an eye on her. But she gets around; she can still do most of her basic personal care. She needs a little help with her activities of daily living, but nothing extraordinary. So as long as she can, she wants to stay at home. She is 87.

Every once in a while, she gets frustrated and says, "I'm just going to sell my house and go into a home." She gets one of those moods. But most of the time she really wants to be home. So hopefully her choice is being honored. And also my sister-in-law gets the benefit of sharing her house. So that's good.

I have to say I sought my mom's advice and shared stories with her more as a child than as an adult. I think it's a normal process, but certainly when I was a small child she was like my best friend. I would tell her everything. But as I got older, and when I got married, I separated naturally from being the super-close child and became a more independent person, Mom and I weren't able to communicate as much. I think for her it was a hard thing, because of the fact that she was a single mom and she invested so much into being a mom. But I think we were always close. She always knew she could count on me, and I always felt I could count on her. Like when Jen was born – our daughter was born with a cleft lip and palate – she was right there for us. When any kind of crisis arose, she was always present and there and wanting to help. And I feel like I provided that same thing to her.

She didn't work in a paid job when I was growing up. She did a lot of volunteer work. When I was in college, she actually worked as a Gray Lady at the Naval Hospital in Philadelphia with the amputees, on almost a daily basis. She was very invested in what she did, and she helped a multitude of Vietnam Vets to adjust to their new physical realities. For me, when I was in high school I was working as a candy striper in the hospital. I always wanted to be a nurse, actually.

I think it was different for my mother than it has been for me when she lost her mother, because my mother's mother was a really difficult person. She was bossy, controlling. She certainly loved us all with a very fierce kind of almost clingy love, but she also was very invasive, especially of my mother's privacy. She was very demanding. My mother was wonderful to her as her daughter, but she was also a big stressor for my mom. My grandmother was a nice person – I don't mean to criticize her entirely – but that's just how she was.

When my grandmother passed away, Ray and I were in Connecticut at the wedding of my half-brother, my dad's son, and my 4 year old daughter Jen, was staying with my mom. My grandmother had a heart attack, so it was totally unexpected. But I think the fact that my mom was taking care of Jen at the time probably made it a lot more difficult for her during her mother's

death process. It happened right while we were at the reception.
Ray actually ended up driving home right away and taking care of
Jen, and I stayed till the next day just because it was my brother's
wedding. I think it was all kind of a weird scenario.

I always had fun with my mom. She had a good sense of
humor, and she was very caring. She was a neat person. I'd like to
end up being half of what she was.

She loved to be with my friends and my brother's friends. They
could feel comfortable talking to her about stuff that some mothers
would hesitate discussing. She wasn't narrow-minded.

My church was helpful to me through this process of losing
Mom. It certainly was a comfort to me. And friends who had already
experienced this loss were helpful.

Walking helps too; I love to walk. I often think about her
when I'm walking.

I have a lot of things that I haven't yet gone through of hers.
I've gone through quite a few things, and I'm trying to give some of
the things away to the grandkids. It's kind of an ongoing project. I
still have some papers that I need to go through. I went through
some as I was getting ready to move. I found things like letters that
I had written to her when I was a child and that kind of stuff.

I don't think there's any one thing that I do that helps me
particularly, because my times of thinking of her are kind of
sporadic and unpredictable. I think I just try to remember who she
was and just savor the memories. I don't have a particular way of
doing that. I never did like the idea of the empty chair at the holiday
table or any of those things. I do maintain a close relationship with
her significant other, and I guess that's the best way I try to honor
her. His daughter – he only had one child – lives down south, so
she can't get up to see him often. So I try to talk to him on the
phone or go visit him. We stay close.

I took him out to her grave after her headstone was placed,
and I took a picture of him touching her headstone. I gave him a
copy. I try to give him some of the comfort, in a healthy way, which
he's missing since her loss. It gives me a good feeling to stay
connected with him, and that's kind of my way of staying in touch
with Mom.

I have some of her things now; as we speak, I'm sitting on a
wicker chair that was hers, and I enjoy having her things around

me. I think of her that way. She actually got into some things like watercolor painting at the end of her life, so I try to have those things around me. She also wrote her memoirs about some of the important times in her life, and we had these copied and gave them to those close to her at the Memorial Service. I would like to do the same kind of thing for my heirs, as they give comfort and are fun to revisit.

To some degree I am aware of how I resemble her, but I don't think I notice it any more than I noticed prior to her loss. In a lot of ways I was kind of a combination of my parents.

Some habits changed. I think I did have a little more trouble sleeping. I don't sleep that well anyhow. But for a while, I think I found myself getting up even earlier than my early, which was very early. And in a way I love that time, because it is a good time, just quiet, so I can really think. I think that was part of the process of adjusting for me.

What I do find, however, is that having had two parents with dementia, I'm constantly kind of on edge that I am going to get it. It certainly has genetic aspects, according to all the studies. I'm on the lookout for my own, sort of monitoring my own behavior all the time. I'm a little fearful about that. I do things like reading or Scrabble to keep my mind active, and I already was doing that before her death. When I do forget things, I worry more about it probably.

I'm well familiar with the five stages of grief, especially having had a child with a birth defect and having had other experiences in life. But I've also found that they don't necessarily occur in predictable ways or in any order. I was prepared for them to just periodically grab me, the way they tend to do at those moments. Then I try to understand them, and to understand that when I have those things happen, that's what it is. Then I know that it will pass, and I can allow them to just be.

I felt that Mom's care was good. I knew her family doctor. I would go to her doctor visits with her as much as I could. Her dental care was difficult, and I think that's typical for the elderly now, unfortunately. Whereas she could see her family doctor right there at Waverly, the dentist wasn't present at Waverly. So I had to get her to her dental appointments, and that was hard for her since she had the terrible mobility issues at the end. And also, it was hard to get an appliance that fit comfortably in her mouth. It's just all that hard stuff about getting old.

Those kinds of things can really affect how someone feels, not only how they function, but how they feel about themselves. So the dental care was a bit of a struggle. I advocated and did what I could, but it was never perfect. The family doctor communicated wonderfully; she would even call me on my cell phone whenever she had a concern and ask for my feedback, which I thought was wonderful. The nursing care at Waverly was very, very good.

But the bottom line is that the impetus to her death ultimately was the fall that she had, and I think no matter what kind of care someone gets, you can't prevent stuff like that. You can't be with someone all the time and have them live in a bubble. Stuff happens. So you can only try to provide the best environment you can. I felt like she had a good environment there. She had a lot of people that cared about her. She especially had this wonderful man in her life, who despite her changes with her dementia, was with her faithfully and lovingly always. So that's pretty cool, and I felt like I did my best too.

Now he's in the skilled nursing part, himself having just gone there over the winter after some health issues. But his mind is just absolutely incredible. He's sharper than most – probably way sharper than me – he's just an amazing guy. He's had to make the transition from independent living to the skilled nursing. He seems to have done so fairly well, but it's still hard.

Thinking about my experience as a mother and my mother's experience, I think we have so many more choices in really every way. And I guess I feel like we have so many more opportunities. I think that had I not worked, I would have really missed out on a lot. I guess our mothers could have worked, but most of them didn't. I think it's a way of really offering an opportunity for success in a totally different non-family way, and it's just a way to expand the horizons and put life in more balance.

I think for my mom she focused so much on being a mother – and sometimes the best mother there was – that she didn't enjoy her own freedom as much as she could have, and that makes me a little sad. Fortunately, she did do so more after I was out of the nest; she actually married twice more after I was married. Unfortunately, both of her husbands got cancer and passed away. And then she had this wonderful relationship with Jack, her significant other. They never got married, but they were just as much of a couple.

As a mother, I'm glad I live now. I'm glad I lived when I did. I feel like I was able to impart to my daughter some of the stuff that I have learned from being a child who came of age during the 1960s.

You know, things are just in general so much more accepted for women. And there are so many more chances. It doesn't mean that you can't do traditional things, because I think that's fine too. But I just think we can be whatever we're best doing and we can still be wonderful mothers.

There's nothing like being a wonderful mother, and there's nothing like being a mother at all, just that whole fantastic gift of being a mother. I was able to be home when Jen was little, and I never would trade that time. That's the thing that makes me sad about mothers today. They miss out on the opportunity to be home in the very beginning in many cases, because of work's demands: leave is still only, if the employer plan is generous, maybe 60 days. I think that's awful. I couldn't have done that myself.

In spite of being divorced and then twice widowed, my mom was always a happy person. She always found the good side of things. I think that was one of her main characteristics that she did teach me, just appreciating life every day.

What advice to offer others going through this? I think it depends very much on the person. I think some people might take comfort in sitting and writing some things down – some thoughts; others wouldn't. Maybe taking some photos of their mother even as things change, and trying to use those photos as tools to get into some realistic understanding that even though the person is different, they are still the same, finding the humanness in that, talking about it, reaching out to others. And trying to take care of yourself through it all.

You have to maintain some compassion for yourself to be supportive of others.

It was really a good experience to talk about this life changing event. Thanks for letting me share!

There is no creation that does not have a radiance. Be it greenness or seed, blossom or beauty, it could not be creation without it.
HILDEGARD OF BINGEN

CHAPTER 13

THE MANY ROLES OF YOUR MOTHER

Let's take some time now to really be with your mother and appreciate all she has been and is to you. It can be a very emotional but also rewarding and healing experience. How did she affect you mentally, emotionally, spiritually, physically, socially, economically, relationship-wise? How are what she taught you, what you watched her say and do, and what you have experienced yourself related to one another? When you have looked at these connections, do you find that you have new choices to consider in your life? There may be things you never thought of that are suddenly on the table to be considered and others which you suddenly realize you would rather discard. This is part of the transformation stage, from tranquility to triumph.

Let's look at all the ways you mother affected your life.

As you read this list, think about what impact your mother had in each role. Go ahead and take some notes as memories or insights come to your mind. This can be a powerful exercise for getting in touch with how important your mother was and why you can't just "get over it," or "snap out of it," but instead can truly benefit and grow from your own awareness and understanding of your mother's contribution to your life.

The many roles of mother

Think of your mother as:

- Source of empowering love
- Healer
- Support
- Manager
- Educator
- Legacy holder
- Protector
- Model as spouse
- Model in life
- Model in love
- Friend
- Worker
- Spiritual mentor
- Policewoman
- Stabilizer
- Disciplinarian
- Confidante
- Community leader
- Provider
- Ruler
- Mediator
- Advisor
- Nurturer
- Cheerleader
- Homemaker
- Collector
- Hobbyist
- Correspondent
- Critic
- Guide
- Instructor
- Cook
- Hugger

- Dresser

You might want to check off the roles which were most important to you or most memorable or most endearing. And remember not even this list is exhaustive. Add others to this list as you think of them. Think what roles she played at these different stages of your life:

- Infant
- Child
- Student
- Teenager
- Young Adult
- Wife/lover
- Mother with children
- Mother with grown children
- Grandmother
- After her death

Notice how your perspective may have shifted in each stage and notice where you are now. Decide also where you would like eventually to be, in your awareness, gratitude, or forgiveness with regard to each or any of these roles or eras of life.

Strategies to keep you on the healing track
Here are a few more strategies which have helped me and others to move through our feelings and reactions:

- Call a relative who shares your loss and share your feelings with them.
- Call a friend who is a good listener with an encouraging attitude.
- Pick up a book by your favorite author.
- Find a website where you can share your feelings in a supportive atmosphere.

- Get outside in nature, with blue sky above, dark earth below, and green, red and yellow around.
- Talk with a spiritual guide such as a priest or minister or other guide who is expert at listening without judging.
- Watch a favorite film.
- Take a glass or two of water – dehydration can cause a lack of energy, a slump in our ability to solve problems, and feelings of fatigue and depression.
- Be physically active, walking, swimming, working out, court games, ping pong, cheering on your favorite team.
- Listen to your favorite music.
- Take up an instrument and make music yourself.
- Sing and dance.
- Attend to self care, with massage, chiropractic, dental care, good eating.
- Breathe deep with long gentle exhalations – the mind works much better when there is plenty of oxygen in the brain
- Write about your feelings.
- Draw or paint pictures of your feelings.
- Leaf through art books or search art websites to find the perfect illustration for how you feel.
- Make a list of the people who remind you most of your mother – it could be her friends, or people you know who remind you of her personality, her favorite hobbies, her most common expressions or phrases, her laugh, or her most cherished possessions.
- Make a list of the movies which most remind you of the kind of relationship you have with her.
- Meet with friends who have experienced the loss of their mothers and share your stories.
- Reread the stories in *Mother Losing Mothers.*

Different strategies will appeal to different people or to the same person at different times. Just be confident that there are always steps you can take to move you forward in your healing and your healthy taking leave of your mother.

Know your own personal tendencies

Since the long ago times when the first known physicians were diagnosing and treating the wealthy citizens of ancient Greece, keen observers of humanity have noticed four basic profiles for the way we handle challenges. These four categories or quadrants are still used every day to categorize folks for employment as well as for psychological analysis. The works of Carl Jung and the Meyers-Briggs matrix are the most familiar versions used today and are both based on these ancient categories. Shakespeare's and Chaucer's characters often speak of and exemplify these four types.

Modern science has begun to identify the biological basis for these tendencies. These four types manifest most distinctly in how we respond to stress. Biologically, each relies primarily on one of the four hormonal groups for their stress response. I won't go into great detail here, but a brief summary may be helpful in demonstrating to you that it is perfectly all right for you to react in your own unique way to the powerful stress of losing you mother.

Some of us tend to react with an aggressive response, taking immediate action and leadership in the situation. These might be called the classic Type A personalities, the choleric types in ancient parlance, known in business as the drivers. Others will be more inclined to withdraw, to need time alone, and to focus on the immediate details of doing what needs to be done. These are most commonly known as melancholic types, known in business as the analyticals. A third group will want to deal with the feelings and relationships involved, to get organized and step back from the situation for the longer view. In classical language these are the sanguine types, didactic and garrulous, known in business as the affinitives. The fourth group will tend to respond with more changeable behaviors but always with a practical dedication to helping others and doing whatever it takes to support them. These are classically known as phlegmatic types, known in business as the supporters.

Each of these four groups will have deep feelings about their loss, but the manifestations of their feelings can play out very differently in each of the seven stages of grief and in each of the activities which surround the death, the funeral process, and the mourning, as well as the everyday activities of the family and career which continue despite the life-altering events of the mother's death.

For example, with such a loss, the sanguine woman might weep often or wax philosophical, while the melancholic woman might seem depressed or unusually energized. The choleric woman might seem angry or highly motivated to take leadership, while the phlegmatic woman might seem impulsive or frustrated, not knowing how she can help. As each moves towards tranquility, transformation, and triumph, their thoughts and direction may look quite different for each. If you want to find out more about this valuable way to understand diverse personalities and their reactions, you will find an in-depth exploration in my book *The Four Temperaments: A Rediscovery of the Ancient Way of Understanding Health and Character.*

An understanding that different people respond differently based on their basic physiological characteristics can help you to appreciate the legitimacy of your own feelings, give you comfort on your path, help you to grow your new relationship with your mother, and also help you to understand and appreciate the different reactions of others.

Think about the richness and diversity among the stories you are reading here. Affirm your own story, and notice that for all, the event is a profound one, and sharing our stories is a great comfort and opportunity for solace and growth.

In the effort to give good and comforting answers to the young questioners whom we love, we very often arrive at good and comforting answers for ourselves.
RUTH GOODE

CHAPTER 14

CAROL'S STORY: SPARKLING GEMS

It is three months since my mother passed away abruptly December 5th, 2009. My father is still living. He's in good health at 72. His days are strange, but we're really close. I have two sisters and the four of us are very bonded.

Since my mom passed away, my father's life has been, I guess, surreal. Even though it's been a few months now, he comes home and she's not there. It's just very hard for him. My mother was a very vivacious and beautiful woman and he loved her very much. They were really in love. They were married 50 years in 2009, and she's just really missed, because she wasn't a quiet, subdued person. She was a firecracker. My sisters and I talk with our father all the time. We get together a lot, the four of us, and it's his favorite thing to do.

My family and I just watched Clint Eastwood's movie named for the car, *Gran Torino.* His wife passes away in that movie too. My father is very much like that character, except my father is religious and not that bitter. There were some similarities there. It was real funny. I told him this morning he should see that movie.

My sisters and I always knew we were close, but my mother being in the hospital out of the blue for a week was a shock. We were all there every day as much as the hospital allowed, and I can't believe how strong we were. We agreed on everything. It was almost like we became one person. It was an awful and amazing experience at the same time.

My mom was never boring. She was a challenging mother in some ways, but she did many things that were really important and good as a mother. For example, she didn't compare my sisters and me ever. She didn't always allow us to be who we were, but she never made us feel like we should be like the other one either. So we were never jealous, we were really supportive. We do anything for each other, and my dad is the same way.

She also never gossiped about others and would remove herself from a situation if others were. She had great character and I too am turned off by gossip by her example.

She was a really, really good mother in that way.

I've changed. I'm almost like a different person since she passed away. I'm not the same person. I went through so much pain. Even with my husband, painful emotions came up that changed so much. I can't believe how much it's changed. I'm like a different Carol. And it was hard. There was a lot of fighting, and we never fight. We are great now, but we went through a crucible, like a furnace, because I changed. I think it's better for him too. Deep down I just had a feeling it was going to be okay.

My dad always said that my mother loved too much. If something happened to us, it was like it was happening to her. Somehow in October, my mother wasn't walking right. Something was different about her all year, but we didn't know what it was, and she wouldn't go to the doctor. We thought maybe she had had a small stroke, but she wouldn't go to check it out. Then when she went finally, her MRI showed that she had some brain issue. It wasn't Alzheimer's, but there was something. She was scheduled to go to a neurologist the day she passed away. So I almost feel like that's when I really lost her. I realized, oh my God, she's not going to ever be the same.

But she was okay. You could definitely have conversations, and we went to the park together. But that's when it really hit me that this is never going to get better. And that's when I changed, October 15th, when I read her results. I've always been insecure about certain things my whole life, and I'm not anymore. I don't care so much what other people think. My mother was always like that. I feel like she left some of her energy with me – like where I was lacking, she put medicine in the wound before she left, not that I would become like her, but that I would heal. And even though she was a tough mother at times, I would take her again, because I like who I am now and I don't think any other mother would have delivered me to where I am, how I've grown.

I didn't go through any kind of depression since my mother passed away. But I miss her terribly, and I can't believe I can't talk to her anymore.

My mother had the self assurance of a 40 year old at 19. She wasn't conceited. I mean, she had hang-ups, but she was really okay with herself in so many ways. And I'm like that now. Just your physical body, for example, she was always okay with her appearance. I have some of the things, some of the "flaws" she had, and she was okay with them. Now I am too.

Even though I always sought her approval, I don't care what people think anymore. I don't even know if that even came from her. It's almost like maybe she just stirred it up in me. I don't even know if it's really about feeling disapproved or not. I think she just had a part in showing me that that's what was going on with me when I used to feel insecure.

She had incredible parties growing up, just incredible. We would have 50 to 70 people. We had this great big barn. It was just so much fun. And all their friends' kids would come. She should have been an actress. She was really very dynamic.

I feel like she showered me with all the good stuff she had in her. It's like she gave it to me – what I didn't have that she had. That's how I feel. What I admired in her, somehow she left it with me.

She was taken to the hospital on a Friday morning and I had seen her on the Tuesday before. We had been at a fair with my two sons, we were sitting at the table, and we were sharing soup. I can't believe that was my last dinner with her – soup! I had no idea. But she did, because she was pulling back socially, majorly socially. And she said something to my kids – I was so struck by it – I just couldn't believe it. I should have known she was saying bye, because she said – and she never ever talked about this – she said, "I have been praying." And she said, "Last night I prayed asking for forgiveness for everyone I've ever hurt."

And she looked at my kids and she said, "I was so hard on your mother. And there are so many things I wish I wouldn't have done."

And I just said, "Gosh, you know, Mom, that's so long ago." And, I mean, I completely had forgiven her, and it's really as if nothing ever even happened. I don't have any bad feelings about it. And I reminded her of what a wonderful and loving mother she was.

Mothers can be so hard on themselves and only remember what they feel they've messed up on.

I was a free-spirit kind of kid. I was the middle of three daughters, and I wasn't a bad child, but I was a free spirit. I wanted to do what I wanted to do, and I guess she worried about that. I guess she worried that I'd get hurt. Now that I'm a mother I can see how you worry about your children. I've read a lot of spiritual books, took from my mother what she did well, and became a good mother myself.

Sometimes I think God gave me sons and not daughters for a reason.

I really love my mother, and I actually talk to her. I ask her for guidance and I kind of feel like she's there. But she's not who she was. She's who we all really are. I feel her essence. And I wear something of hers just about every day, and my sisters do too.

My father wanted us to divide her jewelry among us, which we did with great care. It was the hardest thing we have had to go through of my mother's because jewelry is such a personal belonging. I also get emotional when I recall this day because of how considerate my sisters and I were with each other.

My mother had a living will, but she was on a respirator for a while, for a couple days, just to see if she could pull out of it. When we realized she couldn't, it was definitely a group decision. We were all equal with my dad. He wanted it that way. We realized she couldn't get any better and the respirator was so difficult for her to bear. But we went through ups and downs; she could and she couldn't.

The hospital staff was wonderful. We had no complaints. We couldn't believe that they go through that every day. And they were so compassionate. We were strangers and they were so compassionate. I was amazed.

We think my mom willed it in the end actually, because she didn't want to go down the path she was going to go. She didn't want to lose control of her life. We all think that. And that's what she did. We think that in a way she caused her pneumonia. She would not have been able to go through a long period of dependency.

Mothers from that generation don't want to be a burden, although we all told my dad she could come live with us – we'd take turns. The thing is she wasn't even really at that point yet.

So it was abrupt that she passed away. It was really abrupt. I wasn't there. She moved to the hospice and I came home that morning. But it was less than 24 hours later she passed away, and I wasn't there. My father was there and my older sister. They were the ones who were with her. My older sister lived the closest and she was there to help my dad with getting her to the hospital to begin with.

That night there was a bad ice storm – the night she passed away – and actually she passed away right before the transformer blew in our neighborhood. We didn't have any electricity that night, so we went to Home Depot. It was before Christmas and there we are in a Home Depot. I had already been struggling with James and I was mad at him all the time, but he understood. He knew I wasn't coming out of nowhere. He understood what I was saying and where I was coming from.

But there we were in the middle of Home Depot, just around the same time that she passed away, as we later figured out, and all of a sudden I was overcome with so much love. I had so much love, I didn't know what to do with it. I didn't know where it was coming from. It just overcame me in the middle of Home Depot. I just hugged James right in the middle of the store and people were looking at us like we were strange. But I didn't care. I had so much love for him. Then we left the store and came home, and I got the call that she had passed away.

I don't mind that I wasn't there. I don't mind at all. My time with her was two days before that in the hospital. She came to, and I was alone with her, and that was my time with her.

I didn't have to be there when she passed away. I had to come back to my family. I was gone for seven days and I wore the same clothing for seven days. My sisters remembered. They kept thinking to bring something the next day but they would forget. I just washed everything at night.

My mother was 72 and she looked like she was 50 in the hospital. And the doctors even said, "Is this your mother?" And I said, "Yes, look at her. And she's so sick." She looked so good. And when she passed away, my dad and sister said that she looked like she was 20 and she was glowing. She must have let go of everything. She let go of all the baggage. I just figure she must have got a glimpse of something before she let go to make her body glow.

She lived about an hour north, which wasn't too far. I guess I probably didn't see her enough. But she knew her grandsons well. She and my dad didn't babysit a lot. They did here and there. But she enjoyed it when she did do it. She didn't meddle in our marriages at all. When we got married and moved, she was our best friend. We would get together for family holidays all the time. Everyone.

We went to my sister's house for this past Christmas. It was very strange. But in a way it wasn't really Christmas, because we never had had it at my sister's house; it was always at my mother's house. They always had it. So going to my sister's, it was different, really different. And we didn't make a traditional Christmas dinner. We all just brought hodgepodge of whatever we felt like.

My sisters feel we're almost wandering. I don't feel like I have any specific direction since she passed away. I think I'm wandering in a way, but I'm okay with it. And I'm almost like what I read in a lot of these spiritual books, which say to surrender yourself to God or the universe and things will turn out okay. I feel like I can really do that now. Like it's just coming naturally without thinking.

Before, I thought, how am I going to do that, surrender all my stuff, all my things I'm thinking about? And now I feel like I'm not even trying and that's what I'm doing. I took up ice skating, and I never ice skated before in my life. And it's so much fun. My eldest son and I go skating at Oaks, up Route 422.

I didn't watch the Olympic skating. I haven't been watching TV at all, just watching a movie here and there. I'm reading. My father says he's not doing any reading. He doesn't feel like reading. I am reading, but I'm not watching any TV at all. I never really do.

When I'm skating, I'm just trying to learn how not to fall! I haven't fallen yet, but it is so much fun. It feels so good to skate.

When I started to tell my story just now, I was crying because I felt really close to her just then. Even though we had stuff going on between us, somehow I feel like I was the closest to her, maybe because I was probably the most – she used to say I was the most – like her.

We had really, really deep conversations, and we could talk about anything – she was really open to anything paranormal. And she was really fun. She was a blast. I mean, she was really, really, really fun. She used to let us stay home from school to prepare for Halloween parties and to build things!

She was really wild. She was a wild woman. She was very passionate, and we used to laugh a lot. We used to love to go to Hess Brothers and shop. She just loved buying us clothing, and we'd look at the furs and try them on and dream about having them.

But I really miss talking to her about spiritual things; she was very, very spiritual. She went to church. In fact, she taught Sunday school. My parents both did. And we went to church every Sunday growing up, and that's something I don't do with my kids, although I do talk to them about spiritual things. I don't really want to belong to a church. She was a Christian, but she also really questioned everything. She didn't follow the Christian mold specifically. She wondered about past life but never doubted her belief in Jesus, she once told me. I can talk about all that now with my sisters, but it was neat to be able to talk to my mother about it.

What I was specifically crying about is that my dad told me recently that in her last week she said that I was the only one who brought her up, who made her feel really good. I was thinking, what am I going to tell about my mother? And remembering that just breaks me up.

I didn't know that I did that for her, and I thought, "Gosh, I should have talked to her every day."

She always wanted us to be famous too. She wanted us to be actors or singers or famous artists. She wanted us to be dancers. I took dance when I was a kid, but I didn't really follow through with it.

She was a singer. She sang. And I'd like to take singing lessons. I don't want to be an actress, but I wouldn't mind being a singer.

She wasn't disappointed I wasn't a dancer. She was disappointed I am out of the jewelry business though. She was the reason that I sent my jewelry design portfolio to Bulgari, the owner of the famous company.

My dad was working on Bulgari's cars. He does the pin striping and the gold leaf lettering on his antique cars. Bulgari has over three hundred cars in the area. I got to meet the owner of the shop because of my mother. My mother was always encouraging us. She really pushed us. She didn't keep us back at all. She wanted us to go for things. So I put my portfolio together, and I was really nervous. This was a couple years ago. I was in a funk, thinking I'm not the best artist, so I shouldn't do it at all.

That's where I was at. I can't believe that's how I thought. Somehow, I got it together, I drove up, and I was so excited. The kids were in the back seat. I said, "I can't believe I'm doing this. Can you believe I'm doing this?" Well, they sent my samples to Italy, and the company said, "Well, if you want to design for us, you have to move to Italy because that's where we do it. We don't do it in New York at all anymore."

So that's where it stands. But at least I feel accepted – that I'm good enough to work there.

I have made some changes in my daily routines. I lost 20 pounds and I'm told I'm too thin. I'm exercising like crazy, because I don't want to get a stroke or whatever happened to her. We don't even really know what happened. I exercise every day. I have a stepper or I go for a really long walk or I have a workout tape I do. But every day I do something. And I eat probably half as much as I used to.

Some changes were deliberate and some just happened. I deliberately started exercising, and then I just lost my appetite. I don't have the appetite I used to. The exercising was deliberate because I didn't want to. I thought well, she didn't exercise. I was always trying to help her with nutrition. She did eat salads, but she ate a lot of junk and she admitted it. So I deliberately started exercising like crazy, but the smaller appetite just happened.

Comparing our styles as mothers, what I do that she used to do is I'm really good at making the boys laugh. I can really get down to their level and connect with them and have the same sense of humor. We're always laughing.

And they make me laugh like crazy, where you think your brain is going to split because you're laughing so hard. We've been homeschooling the boys. Definitely homeschooling is something she would have never ever done and she said she could have never done it, but she really embraced it. At first she didn't, but then she really embraced it, because she saw how wonderful they were and how strong their vocabulary was and how mature they were in restaurants and how they pay attention and listen at holidays and pay attention to what adults are saying. She really agreed with what we were doing. And I will always be grateful to Randy and her husband for encouraging us to homeschool. They are truly pioneers.

Lately I've been wondering if they should go to school though. At first it might have been outside neighbor influences. A neighbor might say, "Whoa, they're too sheltered, they're not getting pushed around enough." But they know already how to handle situations. Like when someone is rude to them or is a bully, they just think, "Well, I'm okay, and you're having a bad day, and I'm going to walk away." It's like they don't think it's about them.

I feel they have a lot of qualities which it can take until my age to get. It's like they already have it. I think to myself, "I did not have that quality at your age."

So for parenting, homeschooling is what I definitely did different from my mother. I wanted them to be who they were when they were born and when they were born it just kind of happened. I didn't want them to be told what to do all day long and to stand in line for everything.

I feel like the last two years, even though the boys and I were laughing a lot, I was giving them more time alone than I used to, almost to the point where I feel maybe it's almost too much. I'm letting go, and then I'm wondering if it's a good idea. The funny thing is when you're 14, you are thinking almost like an adult.

I think I'm looking at them more, like really being there, looking at them. Not having my mother here anymore, I think I would like to just sit and look at her and just feel her essence and not even have to say anything, just be with her in the same room.

That's how I was with my husband's father. Sometimes I feel like I should be in the health field. I was very good with him. He had Alzheimer's, and on Fridays his wife would drop him off at my home and he wouldn't talk because of his Alzheimer's. We would sit in the den on the bench seats and we would just sit and face each other.

His wife is very talkative. And so I would just sit there with him, and I wouldn't say a thing and we would look out the window. He had these great sparkly blue eyes, and all of a sudden, he would snap out of it and he would be looking at me. It would happen every Friday the same way.

It's so funny. The same routine. He would look at me as if to say, "Why aren't you saying something?" Not like something was wrong with me. More like, "Why are you not talking? You're not talking at me. You're really just here with me." And then he would start talking! And it was just really neat.

A lot of times I would go to their home to help when he would fall. He couldn't get up and she couldn't get him up. And I would make him help me help him, because I couldn't pick him up either. I would say, "You could do this with me," and I'd look him in the eye: "We're doing this together." Or if he couldn't get in the bed, I wouldn't just tell him what he had to do. I would ask him, "How do you get in the bed?" and then he would do it.

That's how I am too with my kids lately, I think. Since my mom was starting to go through some kind of dementia similar to my father-in-law, I just feel more present with my kids. I wish I could do that now with her and his dad, just be with them.

So I think I'm doing that more. Now, rather than being a "mom," talking at them, tell them to do this, stop doing that, I'm just being with them. For example, if they're on the computer, I'm just in the room with them. I don't even have to be saying anything.

I'm not worried about my mother at all. I guess the way I believe is that she's not suffering. She's not in any way missing us like we're missing her, because I don't think she's experiencing us not being with her.

Spiritually we're together still, even though I guess our ego covers it up. So I'm at peace that I know she is okay. I guess that's why I'm not worried about her. And I don't really believe time exists, because I've kind of experienced it not existing.

I feel like right now, the times I have right now, are more expansive than the times I've had in the last 40 years. They're more expansive. And it's almost as if the last 40 years didn't even happen or it was very tiny, and right now is really big. I don't know how to explain it. I really feel it.

I'm anxious to see what's going to unfold. I'm really looking forward to this every day. Through her, part of me is in heaven somehow.

I remember my grandmother was living with my parents, and she died in their house. She was just old. She died peacefully in the bed.

It was completely different from now, because my grandmother was much older and she just really wore out. She didn't really die of anything specific, and we were all okay with it. It was more like, well, there was nowhere else to go and it was best for her, whereas what happened to my mom was best for her, but we don't know why she had to get what she got so early. So it's really not okay. It was okay that she passed away because she wasn't going to get any better, but it was not okay that she got it so young, it seems to me. I know some people die in their 60s, but she was still pretty young.

Her parents lived long and neither of them had her condition. We don't know why it happened to her. My dad thinks she worried too much and he tells us not to worry.

I absolutely think she was having mini strokes.

I think that is one of the things my mom left me: even though she was the worrier, she left the impression with me not to worry. Just trust life and let go, let go more, rather than trying to control everything. I guess she tried to control the outcome a lot.

The most surprising thing about losing my mother is just how much I miss her. It's really hard. The feeling comes like a song. One thing that's really changed is I am listening to music all the time and I never used to. I'm playing old albums from when I was 13 or 14 on a turntable. Even when I'm driving, I'm playing the radio and singing, and I never used to, ever, ever, ever. I never had the radio on and now I'm always playing music. I don't know if it's to drown out my feelings or what it is. It makes me feel good. My mother liked music. Maybe I will take singing lessons.

Singing is very personal – it's like you're out there naked. You're putting yourself out there more than painting or writing a book. You're really out there.

My best advice for someone facing this process is: don't feel guilty about whatever you're going through. You're yourself. It stirs up a lot of things when you're saying goodbye.

Know that you were meant to be together as mother and daughter. Everything that happened between the two of you was really for the best, even though it might not have seemed like it. Even now, what your mother is going through is just the way it's supposed to be, and you may feel completely numb when she does pass away.

Probably you might not cry at first, and then once all the funeral preparations and all that is over with, then it really gets harder. You'll be surprised how hard it gets then. But then it gets better. Like right now, for me it is getting better, and I feel like she's not dead, just to put it bluntly. I mean, I always knew she wasn't dead, but now I really feel like she's not.

It's more real. I kind of feel her somehow, but it's not the same as who she was. It's her but it's a different kind of her. It's almost like a guardian angel kind of thing. And you know that she knows everything now. All the secrets you kept from her and everything you're doing at the present moment that you wouldn't want her to know or would want her to know, she knows now, but it's okay because she's kind of like God now and she's not judging you.

She's kind of there for you too, because she was your earth mother. She's a little closer to you. In a way she's closer to you than God, because she was your earth mother and you had that experience. But she's also connected to God, so she can almost stream it to you. She can be one path, one stream, one way.

Kind of like the Holy Spirit, like another stream coming to you from God, a more profound one, because she was your mother.

That's how I feel lately. I feel like she's gone, like I can't sit in the room with her, but if I'm quiet I can still feel her.

It's okay with them after they're gone. You realize that it's all okay, that they could have known all along probably. Or maybe not. But now that they know, it's like it's not so bad. It puts a twist of humor in all the craziness, because you realize from their perspective it's all just kind of funny.

That's just what it was, that's all it was.

There's a time when you have to explain to your children why they're born, and it's a marvelous thing if you know the reason by then.
HAZEL SCOTT

CHAPTER 15

THE CREATIVE POWER OF YOUR STORY

Mothers touch every aspect of our lives. There is no more profound relationship than that between a mother and daughter. All future experiences of a daughter are filtered through the filters her mother creates for her before she consciously knows anything is being learned. This profound impact is compounded I believe by the experience of becoming a mother yourself. Your ability to take a second look at your mother-daughter relationship when you yourself are "programming" your little ones is an incredible gift. Whether you have taken advantage of that opportunity or not, another such opportunity presents itself now, with the death of your mother.

Think of the stories your mother told you or read to you as a child. We learn primarily through story and creating our own story with our experiences. Think about the stories you have enjoyed most through your life. Perhaps there are movies, for example, which have had different meanings for you at different times.

A favorite movie of mine which illustrates the profound impact of a mother's death is *The Family Stone*, with Diane Keaton as the mother. She has two daughters in the movie and two sons, and each has a different relationship with the mother. One daughter and one son have children of their own. Each child reacts differently to their mother's impending death. And each is delicately portrayed in their own life situation as they cope with the loss.

Another interesting film about a family which is trying to heal after the loss of their mother is *Everybody's Fine*. Robert DeNiro plays a widowed father who goes to visit his four children around the country and finds diverse receptions among them. His visits set in motion important developments.

Revisit your favorite stories

Now is a good time to revisit stories in literature, film, or art about mothers, family, and love which resonate with your unique feelings and experience and which remind you of your power to heal, to love, and to live with a sense of triumphant joy.

More and more frequently in popular magazines and other media you may find stories about famous women and their mothers. This seems inevitable, since the largest generation in modern history, our baby boom generation, is now going through this stage of appreciating and eventually losing their mothers. For example, around Mother's Day this year, the *Washington Post Magazine* featured Daniele Seiss's story "My Mother's Ashes," about her efforts to fulfill her mother's last wish to have her ashes spread by a special rock in the Shenandoah Mountains.[15] She emphasized the profound effects of the death of a mother.

Magazines want to appeal to the largest market possible, and the largest market is no longer the young adult 18 to 39 when we were dominating the 1980s and 1990s. Rather it is the 40, 50, or 60 something person, who is now taking a longer view of life and perhaps coming to value more their parents and their children and the legacy they are receiving from their parents and giving to their children.

It is worth noting once more that the cartoon films with female heroes which most of us grew up with were about young women coming of age without mothers. Sleeping Beauty had a mother but when she awoke, the castle had been asleep for a hundred years. Cinderella's mother had died, as had Snow White's.

---

[15] Daniele Seiss, "A mother's dying request sends her daughter on an endless search," *Washington Post Magazine* (11 May 2012).

Mothers were distant or absent creatures. We never see these ladies mourning their mothers. Most often, in the fairytales we learned as children, their "wicked stepmothers" were in charge of raising them. It is classic in adventure stories about children for them to be without loving parents. If they had loving parents on the scene, they would never get into so much trouble in the first place.

And that's what our mothers were for us. Most of us didn't have so much drama in our young lives because we had mothers who cared. And now they have gone. The best thing we can do for ourselves is to tell our stories.

Tell your story

Think about the story of your mother and who she was for you because of her life and yours. Share your story with a relative, friend, or counselor who you know can uplift your spirits, listen with understanding, and give you comfort and reassurance. Look for other ways to share your story and new resources from time to time at www.motherslosingmothers.com.

I believe that every human is capable of every feeling. Brain researchers tell us that we are programmed not only to be able to have multiple and nuanced responses to what happens to us, but we are also programmed to be able to empathize, to put ourselves in another's place, in order to sense how they are feeling and how we should respond to them.

If we are capable of all feelings, then something as intimate and global as your relationship to your mother is bound to generate all your feelings at one time or another. They are not to be feared. I found it helpful to make a list of all my feelings. I urge you to give it a try. You may have five, or twenty, or two hundred. It doesn't matter. The subtlety of the human heart is beyond analysis. Let each feeling lead you to a part of your own unique story of you and your mother. These feelings help you to know your story and share it for your benefit and the benefit of others.

The creative energy of a mother giving life to a woman who then becomes a mother herself is one of the ultimate miracles of creation. It is a miracle for which we can be supremely thankful: that as humans we are given a mother who can nurture us to maturity and serve as our model and adviser as we do the same for the next generation. No other species or living thing on earth has this amazingly long and complex relationship. We should respect it, support it, honor it, and cultivate it into the future, with every resource we have as a society.

Explore your spiritual side

I believe that nurturing your own spiritual awareness can help you to accept all that we can never know through science. The more we explore, the more we are in awe of what we do not know. Can a hair on our arm understand all that goes on in our bodies? I think not. But somehow it trusts that whatever is going on is ultimately for its own good. Our relationship with the Infinite is like that, I think. It will remain a mystery. The passing of one generation to the next is a part of that mystery. Children having children creates the infinite on this plane of life.

While God remains a mystery to us, how each of us will participate in God's creation can be a continuing and guiding question in each person's life. This mystery is a comfort if we take shelter in an abiding sense of the magical power of love and life to enthrall and engage us every day.

Not only for ourselves as individuals do we need to give more attention to our personal loss and process of healing. We also must as a society think more about how we really want to have our lives end. We must look long and hard at the ethics, emotion, costs, and benefits of the current approach to medical treatment of the dying.

Increase society's awareness

I would urge that we consider how much more beneficial it might be, for the families they leave behind as well as for their own transition from life, if the dying could be released from invasive medical treatment sooner and be permitted to die at home in familiar surroundings and with their loved ones able to say goodbye. For example, many relatives don't want to bring little grandchildren and great-grandchildren to a hospital, for fear of catching or giving infection or causing too much excitement or concern. At home this is not a problem. Each family can make these decisions for themselves, which can lead the way to a more compassionate approach from the society as a whole.

As a policy matter, we need to ask ourselves whether it is fair to the dying and their families that we draw out the last few weeks or months with medical interventions which diminish the quality of life and drain the family's emotional and physical resources. And there is indeed much more we could do to educate our middle aged and elderly about adjusting their lifestyles to minimize the likelihood of chronic debilitating conditions and to increase the likelihood of vigorous, enjoyable final years.

You can postpone anything but love

The death of my mother has served to strengthen my belief in the power of choice in the moment. This is where our real power lies, as individuals, women, and mothers. In any moment, we can express love by our words or actions, or we can postpone it. It is always our choice. Do we love ourselves enough to eat what will truly nourish us? Do we love the world enough to seek out meaningful work to spend our time on? Do we appreciate enough our influence in the lives of our loved ones to make ample opportunity to show our love? Do we build relationships that really make a difference?

Let your memories guide you and help you to build your future. Your feelings and your memories tell your story. Here is a lovely poem which expresses their value so well.

Memories Build a Special Bridge
By Emily Matthews

Our memories build a special bridge when loved ones have to part
To help us feel we're with them still and sooth a grieving heart.
Our memories span the years we shared, preserving ties that bind,
They build a special bridge of love and bring us peace of mind.

My mother saw the world as profoundly interconnected and knew that her efforts on behalf of those she loved were the most powerful impact she could have for the good of the world. I think I see even more clearly now that the key to a happy life is to spread love all around you.

The most helpful things friends and family can do for a mother like you and me who has recently lost her mother is to love her. Spend time with her, not being sad, but helping her feel her rightness just being her. Ask her to tell her story: moments from her childhood, what was unique or special about her mother, what her mother taught her about being a mother, what the last days or months looked like, what these meant to her and her mother, and what special memories she cherishes of her children with their grandmother. Then just listen, with warmth and appreciation. Be a friend.

My expectation is that my mother will become more and more a part of me. Not that I will become more like her but that her spirit, her energy, will be passed on through me to her descendants and to the world. I don't expect to ever feel that the loss isn't painful, but the pluses of her life for me will more and more clearly outweigh the minuses of her leaving.

I would like to end by saying simply that I am stunned by the glory of a life well lived.

Don't turn a small problem into a big problem – say yes to your mother. Sally Berger

Do Not Stand At my Grave and Weep
By Mary Elizabeth Frye

Do not stand at my grave and weep,
I am not there, I did not sleep.
I am a thousand winds that blow,
I am the diamond glints on snow.
I am the sunlight on ripened grain.
I am the gentle autumn rain.
When you awaken in the morning's hush
I am the swift uplifting rush
Of quiet birds in circled flight.
I am the soft stars that shine at night.
Do not stand at my grave and cry;
I am not there, I did not die.

ACKNOWLEGMENTS

I wish to give my special acknowledgment once again along with my love to the wonderful women who contributed their heartfelt stories to this book. I also want to thank all the great mentors I have had who have impressed upon me when I needed it most the critical value of the mother-child relationship, at all stages of life, and the inherent power of our motherly feelings to guide us naturally in rearing our children. These mentors are too many to mention here. I have interviewed many of them on my net talk radio show *Family First* on the Voice America Health and Wellness Channel. I invite you to listen to their interviews at www.voiceamerica.com. I wish also to thank all my students, workshop participants, counselling clients, lecture audiences, readers, and editors, who have encouraged my work and let me know that the benefits of focusing on happy healthy families are limitless, to individuals, families, communities, societies, and the world. Look for future opportunities arising from this book to tell your own story of the family members you have loved and lost.

ABOUT THE AUTHOR

Randy Colton Rolfe is an author, speaker, family therapist, wife mother, grandmother, and world ambassador for family. She chose her life mission early as a result of traveling with her family in 29 countries before age 20, during 12 summers. She saw both the differences and common desires of all peoples and decided to find out what it took to make families happy and healthy.

She achieved top academic honors at the Shipley School in Bryn Mawr, PA, at the University of Pennsylvania (BA in International Relations, Phi Beta Kappa), at Villanova Law School (Law Review Editorial and Administrative Board), and at Villanova University Graduate School (MA in Theology). She married her college sweetheart John Rolfe, also a lawyer, speaker, and author.

For several years Randy practiced litigation and corporate law with a top Philadelphia law firm (the first woman lawyer ever hired there). Then for the Bicentennial in 1976, she and her husband declared their independence from corporate America and moved to rural upstate New York to homestead and to begin their family. There they loved raising their young son and daughter. Meanwhile they helped the local farmers and Native Americans fight the New York State Power Authority to preserve their land from an ultra high voltage transmission line.

Upon their return to Pennsylvania, Randy helped to develop the legal foundation for carbon trading for the City of Philadelphia. She also earned a Certificate in Applied Clinical Nutrition from the University of Pennsylvania Dental School to round out the health aspect of helping families to thrive.

In 1985 she founded the Institute for Creative Solutions to serve families. She has given hundreds of seminars and guest lectures as well as a number of college courses around the country. She also has had a family therapy practice offering parenting, marriage, family, and nutrition counseling.

Randy became a sought after guest expert on hundreds of radio shows and over 50 major network TV talk shows, including 20 appearances on *Geraldo Rivera,* six on *Sally Jessy Raphael,* and dozens more.

In 1997 Randy joined Nikken, Inc., as an independent consultant, to add Nikken's wellness products and life balance solutions to her offerings to help families to thrive worldwide. You can find unique patented natural health products and an opportunity to help others as an independent Nikken consultant at www.nikken.com/randyrolfe.

For her volunteer work, Randy has been awarded the Chapel of the Four Chaplain's Legion of Honor.

Randy is host of *Family First,* a weekly net talk radio program which airs live on Fridays at 1PM Pacific/ 2PM Mountain/ 3PM Central/ 4PM Eastern, on the VoiceAmerica Health & Wellness Channel. All shows are archived in Randy Rolfe's Content Library for on-demand and podcast download. To access the show please go to: http://www.voiceamerica.com/show/1916/family-first.

Randy is a popular speaker on parenting, natural health, family, and life balance. She has given presentations in Canada and Russia as well as across the United States. She and her husband now reside near Philadelphia, Pennsylvania, and in the Bay Area, California.

Randy's books have been translated into at least six languages. You can get your copies at her website www.randyrolfe.com and at www.amazon.com. This book and most of Randy's previous books are available in eBook format, from Amazon for Kindle and from Barnes & Noble for Nook. You can also read them on your PC, MAC, iPad, iPhone, and Android, by getting a free download of the Kindle app at www.amazon.com or of the Nook app at www.bn.com.

Please visit Randy at www.randyrolfe.com (where you can receive her weekly informative update for free). You can also find Randy on Facebook, Linked In, and Twitter, and at her Blog, www.randyrolfe.blogspot.com. She would love to hear from you!

OTHER BOOKS BY RANDY COLTON ROLFE

The Seven Secrets of Successful Parents

You Can Postpone Anything But Love: Expanding Our Potential As Parents

Adult Children Raising Children: Sparing Your Child From Co-Dependency Without Being Perfect Yourself

The Four Temperaments: A Rediscovery of the Ancient Way of Understanding Health and Character

The Affirmations Book for Sharing: Daily Meditations For Couples (coauthored with her husband John Rolfe)

Princess Buttercup The Cat's Cross-Country Road Trip #3 (coauthored with her husband John Rolfe and their cat)

101 Great Ways to Improve Your Life, vol. 3 (coauthored with David Riklan, Ken Blanchard, and others.)

The True Secret to Weight Loss Is Energy

SAMPLE PRAISE FOR ROLFE'S OTHER BOOKS ON FAMILY

THE SEVEN SECRETS OF SUCCESSFUL PARENTS
WITH FORWARD BY ROBERT E. KAY, M.D.

"This book renewed my faith in my ability to be a good parent." – An Amazon customer.

"I have yet to find a better parenting guide. This empowering book will build and renew your faith. If I could recommend only one parenting book, this would be it." – My Mommy's Place.com - *Mommy's Bookshelf.*

"After ten years of hosting my talk show, Randy Rolfe is one of the best experts to ever sit on our stage. I think this book will benefit every parent who wants a clear, inspiring, and practical guide to success."– Geraldo Rivera, host of *Geraldo Rivera.*

"Randy Rolfe deserves credit for being this generation's Dr. Spock. Mothers and fathers should be issued a copy with the birth of every child. I realize over and over again how right Rolfe's words have turned out to be." – *Main Line Today.*

"A marvel. It has everything. This superbly written work is not just an outstanding parenting book; it's the best book we've ever seen on parent-child interactions." – Denise Breton and Christopher Largent, authors of *The Paradigm Conspiracy.*

"A very good guide to basic, commonsense child-rearing. Highly recommended." – *Library Journal.*

"Rolfe expands with eloquent practicality on such 'secrets' as paying attention and expressing oneself." – *Publisher's Weekly.*

"A big thank you and warm wishes from an appreciative Atlanta reader for your excellent presentation and sharings in this book". – Mike Wilder, Lt. Colonel, USAF (Retired).

"Having this book is like having a wise, experienced friend always nearby." – Ellie Baschoff, mother of six.

YOU CAN POSTPONE ANYTHING BUT LOVE: EXPANDING OUR POTENTIAL AS PARENTS

"The hot parenting book of the season! Worth its weight in gold!" – *Chinaberry Children's Book Service.*

"For parents who would like to raise good kids - a thoughtful book that covers a great deal." – *Washington Post.*

"Solid, inspirational self-help for parents from a spiritual perspective not found in most parenting books." – *Publishers Weekly.*

"This gentle book gets to the essence of what good parenting is all about. It's message reflects the ancient teaching that love is supreme." - *East West Journal.*

"This wise and compassionate book can be of great value to parents who want to build a healthy self-image for their children." – Susan Forward, author of *Toxic Parents.*

"These 165 pages hold a wealth of material. Many of the topics are familiar, some of them I have never before seen in child-rearing literature." – *Mothering Magazine.*

This book conveys a feeling of reverence for childhood while providing workable answers to tough questions. – *Home Education Magazine.*

ADULT CHILDREN RAISING CHILDREN: HOW TO SPARE YOUR CHILD FROM CO-DEPENDENCY WITHOUT BEING PERFECT YOURSELF

"This book underscores a forgotten link in sensitive child-rearing - the parents' own childhood." – *Imprints.*

"Warmly written yet incisive." – *City Paper, Philadelphia.*

"Helps parents change their thinking patterns." – *The Trentonian.*

"This book helped me so much years ago when my children were small that I just was moved to call you now and thank you. I have now passed the book on to my daughter." – Beverly

THE AFFIRMATIONS BOOK FOR SHARING
(WITH COAUTHOR JOHN ROLFE)

"This is a book designed for a couple to read back and forth, nurturing the relationship through affirmations. This is a good tool for professionals and partners who want to develop better communication skills". – *The Twelve Step Times*

"Every page has a message. People carry the books with them or keep them by their bedside." – *The Mercury.*

THE FOUR TEMPERAMENTS: A REDISCOVERY OF THE ANCIENT WAY OF UNDERSTANDING HEALTH AND CHARACTER

"Rolfe's passionate examination of the role and function of the four temperaments in life translates into half handbook, half treatise. Recommended." – *Library Journal.*

"The concept goes back at least as far as the Golden Age of Greece. This book provides useful guidance to living in harmony with one's own nature." – *NAPRA Review.*

"Randy Rolfe shows how to make your natural tendencies work for you." – *Marie Claire Magazine.*

Please go to www.randyrolfe.com or www.amazon.com to place your order.